SPIRIT

COWBOYS, HORSES
EARTH & SKY

ON THE COVER:
Diamond Cross ranch hand P. J. Langmaid crosses the Buffalo Fork River at sunset near Moran, Wyoming.
The ranch sits between Teton National Park and Yellowstone National Park. Photo © Mary Steinbacher

COMPILED AND EDITED BY

C. J. HADLEY

PUBLISHED BY PURPLE COYOTE CORP.

& RANGE MAGAZINE

Golden sunflowers add to the drama and beauty of western cow country. Photo © C.J. Hadley.

"There will never be a time when the old horse is not superior to any auto ever made."

WILL ROGERS, 1832

Publication of this book was made possible by generous donations from people who care about the American West.

PUBLISHER/EDITOR: *C.J. Hadley*
EXECUTIVE EDITOR: *Barbara Wies*
SENIOR WRITER: *Tim Findley*
DESIGNER: *John Bardwell*

Library of Congress Cataloging-in-Publication Data
Hadley, C.J.
Spirit: Cowboys, Horses, Earth & Sky
Caroline Joy Hadley
ISBN 0-9744563-3-0
LCCN 2005907001

Published by Purple Coyote Corp., Carson City, Nevada
All rights reserved.

$39.95 U.S.A.
Printed in Hong Kong

Foreword

COWBOYS, HORSES, EARTH & SKY.
BY C.J. HADLEY

It is in the cadence of a gallop, chatter of a creek, meter of country talk, tattoo of rain on canvas, and the beat of the heart of a horse. It is the rhythm of ranching.

Within these pages you will encounter an elusive but not so subtle West. You will hear its music. You will meet its men, women and children and the critters they care for. You will discover that the labor that sustains those small, clean places is unheralded, unobtrusive and calm, and that this country is better because the cowboys are out there quietly sharing the generations of knowledge they have in this land.

Haunting western images drop deep into memory and pierce the soul. There is the powerful motion of a rider on horseback, the tender bond between cow and calf, the sudden, whirling fury of a high desert storm. It is the sound, sight, smell and taste of the American West. It is her spirit.

Within these pages, if you are willing, you can taste the desolate yet lovely places and share the rugged, arid, and ofttimes painful monster that is the American West.

This book is not romance. It is real and honest admiration for the sustaining traditions of ranching, and for the multi-generational families whose strong hands have kept this place so great.

We can't live out here without a sense of awe and respect. We hope you, too, will feel her embracing spirit and be indelibly branded by our cowboys, horses, earth and sky.

Grays, blacks, buckskins, bays, palominos, roans, sorrels, paints, pintos, appys and mustangs. Colorful cow horses for good cowboys. Photo © Guy de Galard

"Show me your horse and I will tell you what you are."

OLD ENGLISH PROVERB

CONTENTS

Hot storm, Lazy K Bar Ranch near Big Timber, Montana. Photo © Barbara Van Cleve

Dressed as though for a genteel lawn party, this Oregon woman proudly shows the rodent she's just shot. R.W. Heck photo, Burns, Oregon, ca. 1910. Photo © Tom Robinson

R. Marquis photographed three women combing their hair and washing while camping in Wyoming, probably in the early 1900s. Photo © Tom Robinson

> **"In all this wild West the influence of woman is second only in its benefits to the influence of religion, and where the last unhappily does not exist the first continually exerts its restraining power."**
>
> ISABELLA L. BIRD, "A LADY'S LIFE IN THE ROCKY MOUNTAINS" [1873], UNIVERSITY OF OKLAHOMA PRESS, 1960

Stacey Taul, sixteen (left), and Bonnie Gore, fifteen, have already spent years in rodeo barrel racing and roping. Stacey's dad rode bulls and Bonnie's younger brother does, too. Now they are the only teenage girl bull riders on the Central New Mexico rodeo circuit. It's not just exciting, it's a great way to meet boys. Beautifully crafted rodeo chaps, every pair unique, are worn proudly beneath prize belt buckles that attest to their rodeo skills. Photo © Gene Peach

"*Perhaps the spirit of the West is best exemplified in the way it casts aside the unnecessary complications of life. In the mythic West, everyone has an equal start. Justice is simple but effective. We all have the opportunity to start afresh. In these ideals, we approach the heart of the American Dream.*"

GERALD F. KREYCHE, "VISIONS OF THE AMERICAN WEST,"
UNIVERSITY PRESS OF KENTUCKY, 1989

The Muncy family and neighboring cowboys Jimmy Corliss and Mike Harvey ride into the morning fog to gather cattle on the O X Bar Ranch in Torrance County, New Mexico. Photo © Gene Peach

Ranch families

WORDS AND PHOTOS © JAY DUSARD

I didn't grow up on a ranch, but I've always wished that I had. Much of my youth was spent on a southern Illinois farm. That helped. Tractors weren't the horses that I coveted, but they were pretty cool. No livestock to speak of on our place. No four-legged critters to bite me, kick me, buck, stampede, love, hate, frustrate me, die on me, or otherwise educate me. No big country to learn or be thrilled by.

In over forty years of prowling western North America I have met, worked with, and enjoyed the hospitality of many ranch families. To say that all are hardworking, loving, cohesive groups that cherish the land would be unrealistic, untrue. But, I'm hard put to think of any in my experience who don't fit this general description.

A young family may start out at a remote cow camp and later wish to be closer to town when the children reach

Dennis, Deb, Gordy, and Allie Moroney, 47 Ranch, Arizona, 2004. The backcountry of this cow-calf outfit encompasses the north end of the gentle-looking but rough-as-a-cob Mule Mountains. The Moroneys are partners in McNeal Mercantile, where they market natural range-fed beef. It's twenty-five miles portal-to-portal for me to trailer my cow horse and join up with the 47 crew, which I do on a regular basis. I now hate driving past the huge new subdivision slamming up against the 47's boundary fence—the very thing this family left a northern Arizona ranch to avoid. Photo © Jay Dusard

Billie Jo and Earline Goettle and Earl Stucky, Stucky Ranch, Montana, 2003. Three generations take a short break from sorting cattle on one of this Western Slope ranch's lush hay meadows. Earl is aboard his top horse, Blaze, a ropewise campaigner with lots of cow savvy. In addition to guiding hunts for elk, deer, and bear, this family has hosted the best on-location photography workshops that I have ever had the pleasure to teach. Photo © Jay Dusard

school age. Homeschooling may be the answer at this juncture. Multiple generations often work together with obvious advantages, particularly for the young. Sometimes a family member has to hold down a town job to help keep things going. Diversification, such as outfitting and guiding hunts, is sometimes required.

I firmly believe that the key to keeping the open country of the West open and free from the sprawl of development is to keep ranching alive and well. Clearly, the

*Danelle, Dusty, Conner, Bonnie, and Charlotte Crary, Four Seasons Cattle Co., Montana, 2002.
In addition to raising cattle in grizzly bear country, the Crarys run pack strings into spectacular
mountain wilderness areas for guests, hunters, trail crews, and other groups. Photo © Jay Dusard*

Warner Glenn and Kelly Glenn-Kimbro, Malpai Ranch, Arizona, 1996. This father and daughter run two ranches and are internationally renowned hunting guides. Snowy River and Dollar are the mules they rode on the day Kelly jumped the wild jaguar that Warner ultimately caught up with, photographed, and wrote about in "Eyes of Fire: Encounter With a Borderlands Jaguar." The Glenns, including Warner's wife, Wendy, are active founding members of the Malpai Borderlands Group, which has a ten-year history of bringing together ranchers, environmentalists, scientists, and government agencies as collaborators in preserving an extensive "working wilderness." Photo © Jay Dusard

family who savvys, manages, protects, and improves their rangeland is on the right track. The modern ranch family can no longer do it all with horse and rope, given the complexities of regulations, agencies, critics, markets, and inflation—not to mention coming up with a sound strategy for preserving the outfit and its way of life for succeeding generations.

*   *   *

Imagine a video game with a steep, brushy, boulder-strewn mountainside and cows and calves scattered in inaccessible places. The objective of the game would be to bring all the cattle together and down to "the drive." Way cool in a mall arcade somewhere. But some ten-year-old ranch kid is going to be up there on a trusted horse dealing with a reality that isn't exactly virtual.

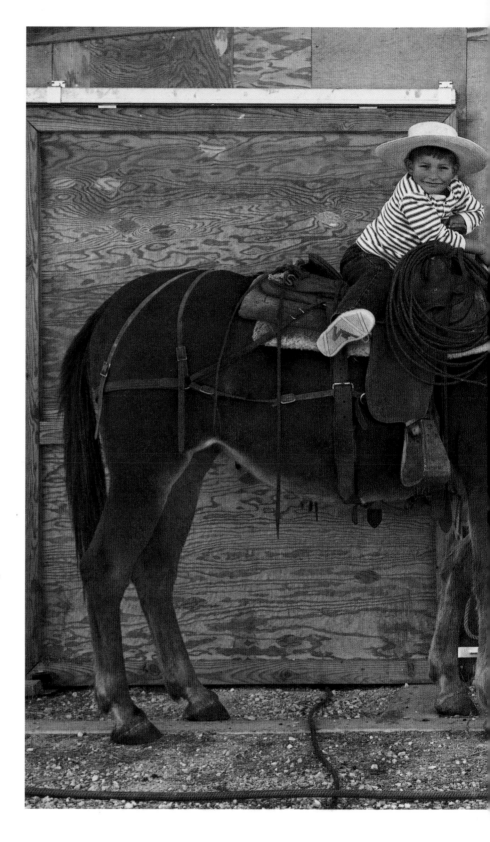

Photographer Jay Dusard lives near Douglas, Arizona, where he breeds quarterhorses, punches cows, and plays jazz cornet. Signed copies of "HORSES," © 2005, may be purchased directly from Jay. E-mail <jbard@theriver.com> or call 520-364-7440.

Joe, Bob, Mary Lou, and Michael William Coffelt, Rafter Cross Cattle Co., California, 2002. A former photo student of mine showed me a great action shot of Bob Coffelt, mounted on a dandy mule, throwing a perfect head loop onto a running calf at a neighborhood branding. I wasted no time in tracking down Bob and his fine young family and, of course, the celebrated mule Peaches. Photo © Jay Dusard

Dick Cofield, Jim Prewett and Dick's son Richie gather Redfern Ranch cattle for branding at Landrum Camp, Gilroy, California. One of those pushing the cattle is manager Jim Prewett's young daughter Althea. Here in the coastal hills, ranching neighbors are always happy to help. Photo © Heather Hafleigh

Soft light and a calm morning braid a reflection of Jeff Bourdet's cattle in a man-made lake on the Rancho La Chiquita in Gilroy, California. Among those riding with second-generation rancher Bourdet are his sons Carson and Cody, and daughter Aimee. Photo © Heather Hafleigh

"I think our governments will remain virtuous for many centuries: as long as [the people] are chiefly agricultural, and this will be as long as there are vacant lands in any part of America. When they get piled up upon one another in large cities, as in Europe, they will become corrupt as in Europe."

THOMAS JEFFERSON TO JAMES MADISON, 1787

Time out

George Washington played billiards. The billiard table John Quincy Adams installed in the White House was decried as "gambling furniture." German-Swiss-born Cincinnati carriage builder John Brunswick encountered his first billiard table at age twenty-six and immediately set out to build ornate tables, today considered priceless works of art. Like the amazingly elaborate Brunswick back bars which graced saloons in the West, the Brunswick tables, cues and other equipment were meant to be used. Some still are in use today. For the men of the West (few women would enter a pool hall), a game of pool was another test of skill, but also a time to relax, away from the endless daily chores.

Brian Morris worked as cow boss for the Circle A in Paradise Valley, Nevada. When asked many years ago whether the buckarooing was good in Nevada, Morris told the young cowboy: "It's good if you don't want to get rich, can take a lot of abuse, and don't mind getting old awful fast." Photo © William Albert Allard

The way it is and the way it was. Photo © William Albert Allard

Twelve men and a boy assembled for photographer John McMullen in front of The Globe Saloon in Drewsey, Oregon, ca. 1900. "Baths" are the next-door business. Known cowboys: second from right, Morgan Presley; third from right, Leslie Riley; seventh from right, Bill Norton. Photo © Tom Robinson

Equus caballus

BY JOEL NELSON © 2002

I have run on middle fingernail through eolithic morning
And I've thundered down the coach roads with the revolution's warning
I have carried countless errant knights who never found the grail
I have strained before the caissons and moved the nations mail

I've made knights of lowly tribesmen and kings from ranks of peons
I've given pride and arrogance to riding men for eons
I have grazed among the lodges and the tepees and the yurts
I have felt the sting of driving whips and lashes, spurs and quirts

I am roguish—I am flighty—I am inbred—I am lowly
I'm a nightmare—I am wild—I am the horse
I am gallant and exalted—I am stately—I am noble
I'm impressive—I am grand—I am the horse

I have suffered gross indignities from users and from winners
And I've felt the hand of kindness from the losers and the sinners
I have given for the cruel hand and given for the kind
Heaved a sigh at Appomattox when surrender had been signed

I can be as tough as hardened steel—as fragile as a flower
I know not my endurance and I know not my own power
I have died with heart exploded 'neath the cheering in the stands
Calmly stood beneath the hanging noose of vigilante bands

I have traveled under conqueror and underneath the beaten
I have never chosen sides—I am the horse
The world is but a player's stage—my roles have numbered many
Under blue or under gray—I am the horse

So I'll run on middle fingernail until the curtain closes
And I will win your triple crowns and I will wear your roses
Toward you who took my freedom I've no malice or remorse
I'll endure—This Is My Year—I am the horse

Equus Caballus was written in the autumn of the Year of the Horse, 2002. Eohippus was the earliest known ancestor of the horse showing up in the Eocene deposits going back fifty million years. With four toes front and three behind, he finally became Mesohippus with three toes on all feet. Equus had evolved by the beginning of the Pleistocene and by this time the middle digit had become the hoof with the side digits diminished to what we call the splint bones. And so we see him now running on middle fingernail.——Joel Nelson, cowboy, poet, horseman

Playful geldings at the O6 Ranch in West Texas. Mounts have already been selected from the remuda for the day's work. These were turned loose so they decided to dance in the dust.
Photo © Diane Lacy

Arizona dream

WORDS © DODIE ALLEN. PHOTOS © CARTER ALLEN.

If you want to bring a twinkle to her blue eyes or a warm glow to her face, just mention family or ranching to Grace Wystrach. Her sprawling ranch house just east of Sonoita, Arizona, is filled with photos of her six children—four daughters and twin sons. Windows frame a sweeping view of rugged mountains and high desert grasslands. This is home, where Grace planted her heart when she was only nine years old.

Usually clad in jeans and a shirt, Grace says in matters of style her daughters claim "her give-a-damn is busted!"

Spring calving is Grace's favorite time as she welcomes each new calf to her purebred Hereford herd. Time off was rare. "Piling my children into a big truck and pulling ten head of cattle to shows from West to Midwest, culminating with the American Hereford Association National Show, was our annual vacation."

Today she sells bulls at two Arizona sales each year. Even though it's still mostly a man's business, Grace has earned the respect of buyers in the Southwest and Mexico.

Born Grace Townsend on a ranch near Marfa, Texas, she has fond memories of riding in the pickup with her dad, singing "Home on the Range" at the top of her lungs. They moved to Colorado when she was five. Tears streamed down her face as they turned off their last Texas windmill.

Grace admits she hates to leave anything.

During the Depression, the Colorado ranch doubled as a guest ranch along with the cattle operation to make ends meet. Her mother, Elizabeth Benciger Townsend, was the head wrangler and a

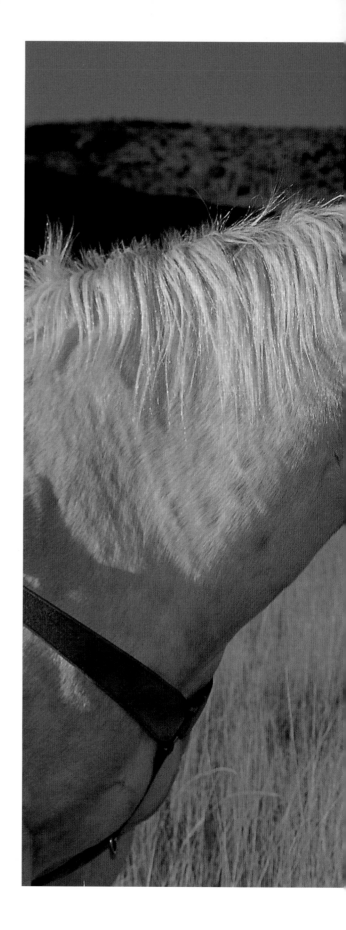

A neighboring rancher says that Grace "rides like the wind and usually on a horse with a lot of get up and go." He says that if you think you work hard, just ride along with Grace for a day and you'll find out what work is. Photo © Carter Allen

Most guys would get tired just trying to follow Grace around. Her dad didn't ask her to come to brandings and gatherings: he expected her to be there, mounted and ready at first light. Photo © Carter Allen

"tough little woman" who taught her daughters a solid work ethic along with good manners. A few years later, the Townsend family bought the Rain Valley Ranch and settled in Arizona's prime ranch land.

With her two sisters, Grace attended St. Joseph's Academy in Tucson followed by the University of Arizona. Each weekend the girls were expected to be in the saddle helping with ranch chores. Summers were spent riding all 18,000 acres checking some 300 head of mother cows for screw worms. The Townsend gals got suntans at the same time, riding in bikinis!

Grace's first teaching job was in Garden Grove, California, close to El Toro Marine Corps Air Station. There she met a handsome pilot, Michael Wystrach, who was to become her husband. They made a good team. Mike heads the entrepreneurial branch of the family, managing several gas and convenience marts along with The Steak Out restaurant and the Sonoita Inn. Each of the Inn's eighteen rooms is named for a local ranch and displays its history and a branded door. Grace is a willing hostess at the restaurant when needed and loves people, "But I also love to be alone, working on the ranch."

For Mother's Day, her daughters surprised her with a framed collection of her famous expressions. "Lazy is a Four Letter Word" prompted one daughter to announce that it isn't a sin to get up past five a.m. or take a nap. Grace firmly believes that all animals no matter how small or ugly are creatures of God. She has taught her children to "always believe in something greater than yourself."

"All men should be shipped away and brought back only for moving" is a favorite tease for her sons. Grace is certain "there is nothing that a long ride or long walk won't make sense of."

Five grandchildren, four girls and a boy, now bless her life. Grayson, age seven, calls her "Moo."

"Moo, when you are tired of the ranch, will you give it to me?" the little girl asked recently. "Will you give it to me?"

Looks like the same blood runs in her veins.

Pitchfork Ranch cowboys in West Texas gather at the chuck wagon for supper as an evening thunderhead rolls over the wagon. Photo © Bob Moorhouse

As we loaded the horses into the truck for the return to the ranch I asked Mackie how he liked this kind of work. He looked at me. His shirt and the rag around his neck were dark with sweat, his face coated with dust; there was a stripe of dried blood across his cheek where a willow branch had struck him when he plunged through the brush after some ignorant cow.

"Look at yourself," he said. I looked. I was in the same condition.

"I do this only for fun," I explained. "If I did it for pay I might not like it. Anyway you haven't answered my question. How do you like this kind of work?"

"I'd rather be rich."

"What would you do if you were rich?"

He grinned through the dust: "Buy some cows of my own."

EDWARD ABBEY, "DESERT SOLITAIRE," SIMON & SCHUSTER, 1968

A long neck and keen eyesight help the eagle find a meal. Long legs allow the bird to dip lethal talons deep into water for its prey. Massive wings let the eagle "rest" on a thermal current, riding on the air to conserve energy. Photo © Eberhard Brunner

On wings of freedom

PHOTOS © EBERHARD BRUNNER.
WORDS © BARBARA WIES.

Our national bird, the bald eagle, is the only eagle unique to North America. Their white heads ("bald" is an obsolete term for "white") distinguish them from other eagles. Known as raptors—the same root as "rapture"—eagles are birds of prey that kill with their sharp and powerful talons. Fish are an important food source. The slightly larger female has a wingspan from seventy-two to ninety inches. Eagles live from fifteen to twenty years and they mate for life.

Although found over most of North America and in northern Mexico, most prefer the northwest Pacific Coast, where salmon are abundant. About half of their number live in Alaska, where these were photographed.

Soaring gracefully from thermal to thermal to keep their large bodies aloft, eagles have always inspired dreams of flight

and freedom, strength and longevity. In all parts of the world, eagles are creatures of myth and wonder. With eyes so large they must rest in immovable sockets, eagles scan by turning their heads almost completely around.

Ancient Greeks believed eagles were the only creature able to stare directly into the sun. Native Americans revere the eagle and use its feathers (there are 7,000 on an adult bird) in religious ceremonies.

Once considered endangered, eagles may soon be removed from the "threatened" list. But they will always be protected by laws that make the use, sale, possession or trade of eagle feathers or parts illegal to all except by special permit to Native Americans who honor them as sacred.

Mealtime is anytime an eagle finds prey. Fish are preferred, salmon especially. Like this bird, about half of the world's bald eagles live in Alaska. Photo © Eberhard Brunner

A dark beak and brown feathers mark this as an immature eagle. When fully grown, the scissorlike beak will be golden, the head and neck feathers gleaming white. Photo © Eberhard Brunner

Branding time in Curlew Valley

WORDS AND PHOTOS © RICHARD MENZIES.

"It's the kind of a place where you can sit on your front porch and watch your dog run away for three days."

—COLEN SWEETEN, COWBOY POET AND RANCHER

Over the past hundred years, the population of Curlew Valley has trended steadily downward. The windshield view from U.S. 84 is long and unobstructed, with very few trees or houses for runaway dogs to hide behind. However, there is a verdant blanket of ground cover, thanks in part to a wet spring—thanks even more to the families who tend this land.

Grouse Creek Jack, an Indian who lived in the area for a hundred years, remembered the valley as a sea of waving grass teeming with deer, elk, antelope and buffalo. Then came the iron horse and Charles Crocker, a Central Pacific railroad promoter and wannabe cattle baron, whose Promontory Ranch Company eventually grew to encompass fifty square miles and 45,000 head of cattle. But the big winter of 1886-1887, followed by three years of drought and still another big winter, wiped out most of Crocker's herd and put a big dent in the wildlife population. By the 1890s, Curlew Valley was pretty much covered with sagebrush and bones.

Half a dozen local ranchers subsequently bought

Rick Steed gathers his loop for the next catch of a calf's back feet. Working on the ground are a couple of weekend cowboys helping rancher Tim Keller (kneeling on right), who is tagging ears, giving shots, and castrating the bull calves. Photo © Richard Menzies

Chowtime around the Dutch ovens of Rod Arbon, cowboy cook (who would rather be roping). Rancher Ross Junior Anderson, called "June" to his friends, knows there are no stumps or rocks to sit on on the Curlew Flat so he brought a dozen plastic chairs for a little comfort on the range. This action was much appreciated. Photo © Richard Menzies

out Crocker's grazing rights and have worked together ever since to rehabilitate the far northern Utah rangeland.

"These cattle you'll see today are in as good a shape as any cows you've ever seen, and they haven't been fed a bit of hay," explained my guide Colen Sweeten. "But these ranchers save that pasture during the summer. They let the grass grow up and go to seed. In the winter when it's damp, the cattle will eat that dry bunchgrass. They will also eat quite a bit of that curly sage and they come outta there going strong. And when the snow goes off, there's crested wheatgrass and other early grasses that'll put them in good shape by the first of May when they have to go to Idaho.

"This particular area doesn't get a lot of snow, and when it does, it doesn't stay too long. It's good winter range, but it didn't work for the

Fifth-generation cowboy, Cutter Eliason. His dad runs cattle on Curlew Flat at the north end of the Great Salt Lake. Photo © Richard Menzies

From left: Russell Boyer, Jess Daniels, Lynn Anderson, Wendy Boyer, Don Eliason and Dave Showell. Below: Don Eliason, right, and his son Ken. More cowboys are ready to ride because Ken and wife Kristy have five sons. Photo © Richard Menzies

Promontory livestock because there was no feed left after they'd pastured it in the summer."

At Molly's Café in Snowville, Colen and I hooked up with Rod Arbon, who offered to give us a lift in his battered pickup to the spot where the annual spring branding was underway. Rod's truck towed a trailer heavily laden with cast-iron Dutch ovens and propane burners. We were soon joined by a second high-clearance 4x4 whose bed was heaped high with nesting patio chairs. Colen and Rod became visibly excited, insofar as two old cowboys are capable of exhibiting visible excitement.

"This is about the third generation of these ranchers who've stayed together and they get along fine," Colen explained. "They run their cattle together and, when they brand, they just run three or four hundred head of cattle in a corner, hold 'em there, go in and pick out their own calves and bring 'em up to the fire and tell 'em what brand to put on."

At the branding corral I was introduced to half a dozen sturdily built stockmen, each with a handshake firm enough to crack walnuts. Ross Anderson, Don Eliason, David Eliason, Jess Showell, Carl Steed, Ken Keller—a consortium of stockmen, each with his own grazing allotments and each with his own brand. Teenagers stoked the branding fires and tended the irons, and it was fairly easy to guess which youngster belonged to which adult. But to me the calves all looked alike. How in the heck do they determine which calf belongs to which rancher?

"Well," explained Colen, "a calf will suck any cow, but a cow will only let her own calf suck her, so they just quietly ride in the herd and if they see a calf that's gettin' its dinner and the cow doesn't object, they can be pretty sure that's her calf, and they read the brand that's on her and drag it up to the fire and tell 'em what brand to use."

Of course, roping a specific calf by the hind hooves and extracting it from the milling herd requires a good horse and extraordinary skill with a lariat—just as castrating and marking require a strong stomach.

By and by the crew broke for a hearty lunch at Rod Arbon's chuck wagon. I, of course, was first in line. Although I tried hard to blend into the crowd, it was patently obvious to those sharp-eyed cutters that the conspicuously clean person who had come to dinner wasn't a real cowboy but just another useless journalist.

"It's hard work," allowed Colen. "Sometimes it's hard to show a profit, but there's something about growing up on the land and having an interest in it that doesn't get out of your blood."

Clayton Eliason shows his brothers his roping technique. Photo © Richard Menzies

Tools of the trade: a sharp knife, vaccine guns, and an ear tagger. Photo © Richard Menzies

"Alpine Saddler," watercolor © 2003, private collection

William Matthews

"I have always been interested in people who live on the land and are sustained by it," the artist says. "I'm drawn to the natural contrasts: hot and cold, wet and dry, light and dark, straight and twisted, smooth and textured. These are the elements necessary for a great painting."

Hailed as the new Remington, Matthews' work has been called a subtle philosophical study of western ranch life. "I prefer mystery," he says. "I don't want to tell the whole story or be direct."

William Matthews' work can be found in many exhibitions and in public and private collections. In addition to the William Matthews Gallery in Denver, his work can be viewed at the Spanierman Gallery, New York, and the Nedra Matteucci Fenn Gallery in Santa Fe.

William Matthews Gallery, 1617 Wazee Street, Denver, Colorado 80202, 303-534-1300 <www.williammatthewsgallery.com>.

"The Roper," watercolor © 2003, private collection

"A Fresh Pony,"
watercolor © 2005,
private collection

A good life at Roaring Springs

WORDS AND PHOTOS © LARRY TURNER

"I wouldn't trade this way of life for anything," says Roaring Springs Ranch manager Stacie Davies. "This is heaven for raising a family. The boys learn responsibility and the value of accomplishing something every day. This sets them up for life. It's important to learn the value of hard work and responsibility."

In a country that continues to become more urban, Stacie, wife Elaine and their six sons are a solid rock of traditional family values: hardworking, cooperative, honest, honorable with their words and promises, dedicated to the health of their community and their profession as ranchers.

Historic Roaring Springs Ranch nestles against the Catlow Rim of southern Steens Mountains, an isolated glacial-carved range in the southeast part of Oregon. The name comes from the 7,000-gallon-a-minute springs flowing on the hillside near ranch headquarters, once part of Pete French's vast cattle empire of the 1880s.

Owned by the Bob Sanders family from Washington state, the 600,000-acre range is vibrant and productive. Roaring Springs is unique in having a full-time wildlife biologist on the payroll, sponsored by ranch cattle dollars.

"We are ecologically very sound," Davies says. "Our projects always benefit wildlife and sustainable foraging vegetation is ninety-five

Stacie Davies and the Roaring Springs buckaroos take a break while driving almost a thousand head of cattle away from Catlow Rim. Opposite: Stacie and the crew move cattle through the gate into new ungrazed range closer to the home ranch. Photos © Larry Turner

percent native plants. We could survive without fossil fuels."

Wildlife is abundant, proving that healthy livestock (500 mother cows and 150 horses), wildlife and plant communities can exist together. The sage grouse population is exploding due to native forbs management practices. The forbs—essential to the sage grouse chicks' diet—come as a result of land disturbed by cattle and fire.

"The truth about successful grazing makes hardcore environmentalists who wish to purge the West of grazing uneasy," says Davies. "They're in the business of raising funds through controversy. They can pick on cow pies because they're not attractive. However, they fail to tell the positive results of grazing and its benefits to land and wildlife."

Davies is dedicated to environmental health. "We care for the land like we care for our children. If we disrespect it, we get no respect. Nor do we get good results. Nature and animals can be unforgiving."

The range at Roaring Springs is very much as it was when man first came on the scene. Native plants thrive. Wildlife is abundant, including deer, antelope, rabbit, coyote, bighorn sheep, raptors, sandhill cranes, waterfowl, upland birds, badgers, marmots, squirrels, wild horses and elk.

Roaring Springs works with master's and doctoral students of Oregon State University. They use the ranch as a laboratory. The ranch provides housing and meals in the cookhouse with the ranch crew. "They are allowed to do experimental projects that we all learn from," says Davies, "such as

the utilization of grazing winter scrubs without harm."

Roaring Springs Ranch is a member of Oregon Country Beef, a family ranching cooperative which raises natural beef without hormones and antibiotics. Calves are treated humanely in an environmentally sound manner and fed healthy diets.

The six Davies boys—Zed, Wes, Dallen, Erik, Jeff, and Scott—help out on the ranch along with two buckaroos, one cook, a maintenance man and

a farm crew.

"All of the boys are responsible for certain chores," says Davies. "Morning chores are at six a.m., breakfast at seven, then they're off to school." Kindergarten through eighth grade is fifteen miles away. The high school boys stay at Crane Boarding School, seventy-five miles away, coming home for weekends when they don't have athletic events. Sunday, they all go to church together.

Elaine is on the local school board and active in PTA and 4-H. Once a week, she drives her junior high boys and neighbor kids 150 miles round-trip for football practice.

"Our life is full," says Davies. "Elaine wants to leave a legacy of helping to make her kids and other kids better citizens. I want to be remembered as being a good citizen, husband, dad and a contributor to this life. The love I have for family sustains and inspires me every day. I have a deep love for God, country and this ranch, too."

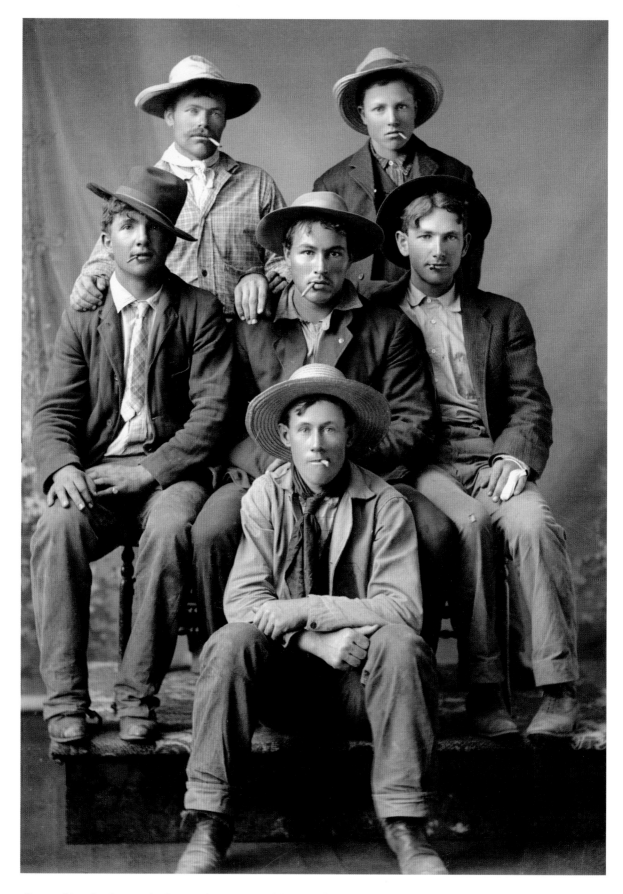

Six smoking buckaroos in Burns, Oregon, ca. 1900. The fellow on the left with the tilted hat is Dole Smith. He was identified by his granddaughter. Smith owned a ranch near the Five Mile Dam on the Silvies River in Harney County, Oregon. He was born in the 1880s, and was probably around twenty years old when photographed by John McMullen. He died in 1965. Photo © Tom Robinson

"There is an easy comfort given to believers of the Western dream, knowing that cowboys are, at this very moment, galloping around somewhere, roping sick stock, and sleeping out under the stars. Why this kind of trivial knowledge should make a difference in anyone's life is a mystery."

KURT MARKUS IN "BUCKAROO," NEW YORK GRAPHIC SOCIETY, 1987

The Edsall family near Avon, Montana. Left to right: Merle, sons Roy and Clayton, wife Sharon. Clayton was in a funk. His mother was at him to step up for his portrait. I suggested that he should be in the image wherever he wanted. He went over and plopped himself on the wood box, seemingly relieved to be given his choice. I made the image, finding just what I was looking for. I find it fascinating, when making portraits, how each person expresses individuality with both dress and carriage. Photo © Charles W. Guildner

The shadow on the cutback

BY JOEL NELSON © 1988

Hist'ry wrote his epitaph
When barbed wire cut the range
While he was but an embryo
Adjusting to the change.

But he was not aborted
By the creaking stretch of wire,
And the numbers still are legion
Of the horseback man for hire.

His shadow cast at sunrise
On some cutback wall of sand
Is a mate to the conquistador's
In Coronado's band.

He is steeped in the traditions
Of those horsemen long ago.
He is rumored to be mortal
He will not admit it's so.

Since the glory that was Camelot
With her dragons breathing fire
The hero of the world has been
The horseback man for hire.

And his glory days aren't over
In spite of all we've read.
He is no less than he ever was
In spite of what's been said.

In the deserts of the high-tech world
He is trailing up his cattle
He will never quit his horses
And he'll never sell his saddle.

JOEL NELSON WROTE THIS AS A HORSEBACK
MAN FOR HIRE AT THE 06 RANCH IN TEXAS

Like generations of his family before him, fourteen-year-old Ventura Trujillo rides out on New Mexico's splendidly hued Ghost Ranch. Photo © Gene Peach

Prey & hunters

When you live out in the country, sooner or later you're bound to come face to face with one of the critters. If you're downwind and follow your instincts to just stand still, it's almost always a show produced by nature, directed by God. And if there is no need to feed yourself or protect your family, you feel almost a part of them.

I wonder sometimes if in those deep shadows of the trees they don't now and then pause to watch us in just the same way.

TIM FINDLEY, 2005

It took Montana's Swanson Ranch kids five or six hours to catch this baby prairie dog. They led it around in a halter then let it go, back to its burrow, none the worse for wear. Photo © Cynthia Baldauf

Stadheim Ranch sheep enjoy morning sun in southwestern North Dakota. The Stadheims run cows and sheep like many ranchers on the hilly, dry border of North and South Dakota along the North Grand River. Photo © Carrie Longwood

Gray wolf mother and pups, northwest North America. Play is aggressive—and meant to be. These are predatory carnivores that will kill for food and fun. Photo © Joe McDonald, Tom Stack & Associates

A whitetail fawn browses on the Montana National Bison Range. Eyes and ears are alert for the approach of a predator, and mother is certain to be hovering nearby. Pretty white spots resemble the dappled sunlight of spring. It is camouflage for the youngster. Photo © Cynthia A. Delaney

A colt with some heart © CAROLYN DUFURRENA

There were six working cattle ranches around Nevada's Pine Forest Range in the 1980s. Of those six ranches, one is bankrupt; the one Merv worked for has sold its cow herd and been transformed into a private golf course; another runs only lease cows and is in the process of selling its private land in the high country; and another has evolved into a base camp for guided hunts. Those ranches which still run cattle do their best to keep them out of the way of the tourists. Fishermen and hunters now flock here in their season, to the place where this day passed in 1984. It is a Wilderness Study Area; a Bureau of Land Management Backcountry Byway runs around it. There will be few opportunities in the future for working cow horse colts to meet fly fishermen at Blue Lake. It was a passing moment, two cultures just touching, before one passed into history.

The summer afternoon passed slowly, thunderheads drifting over the Pine Forest Range in northwest Nevada. Peggy sat at the kitchen counter, coffee and a cigarette in front of her as we talked and talked the hours away. The little boys, my son, her grandson, played in the shallow ditch just outside the window, making endless mud pies. I watched while Peggy folded laundry. She made yeast rolls and set them on the pilot light to rise. She put the laundry away. We had another cup of coffee. Merv was only a little late. It wasn't near time to get worried. Still, her blue eyes scanned the ridge every few minutes.

Merv snaked the big bay colt down over the rocky, brush-choked trail, through the lightning-blackened pines rimming the cirque's headwall ridge, down slopes thickly masked by mountain mahogany and aspen. The trail had led him from the headquarters west, up a rocky canyon, across a big high meadow, a little soggy even this late in summer, and up again, out of the sagebrush and into the pines. He had a pretty good scatter on the cattle, fifty head in this little basin, fifty head over there. There was room on this mountain for a lot of cows. It was a good place to get a horse started, and he was happy with this one.

The lake is dark green at midday, and green light brocaded the jumble of granite boulders beneath the surface. He stepped off in a grassy place near the sparkling glacial lake and cautiously slipped the hobbles around the colt's hocks. He stood, and stretched. He walked to the shore through the skiff of long pine needles over fine sand.

Swifts skimmed the wavelets, hunting the afternoon hatch. The wind freshened. The grizzled cowboy breathed, lifting the terrible, old, used-to-be-white hat off his forehead.

A couple of fly fishermen eyed him curiously, a figure out of a western novel riding into the twentieth century. The fishing population here had changed since the trail had been closed. Used to be you'd know at least some of the crowd, but nowadays it was a hike-in deal. Not many locals came up here anymore, and these men were from someplace else. One of them came over.

"How's the fishin'?" Merv inquired politely, fishing his own can of Copenhagen out of a blue shirt pocket. They discussed the merits of angling in the middle of the day, dubious at best, and shot the breeze for a while. The fisherman said he'd better work his way around the backside.

He eyed the bay, half asleep in the warm sun as he passed by. "What's your horse's name?"

"Roller."

Merv did not explain to this man how the horse had earned his name. The colt loved his life, loved his work. He loved to chase cows, and worked up a pretty good sweat doing it. When the saddle came off at the end of the day, he would roll and roll in the pasture. "As many as six or seven times," Merv would tell me later.

"Nice horse," the fisherman commented, walked past, and smacked him on the rump.

Merv's eyes widened as Roller—still hobbled—came out of his doze with a snort. He took one, then two sideways jumps toward the lake. Merv moved as carefully as he could toward the colt's head, but Roller was panicked, and too quick. Every yank on those hobbles scared him worse. Next thing Merv knew, Roller had bucked himself, saddle, snaffle bit, hobbles and all, into the icy green water.

Glaciers carve a steep profile, and the water is deep close to shore. The terrified horse lunged, struggling for his life. The hobbles kept the colt's front hocks close together: handcuffs. Waves surged from his shoulders as he heaved against the weight of the soaked saddle and

the cinch and slid the sopping saddle to the ground.

For a while he didn't say anything. Then, "Well, hell, Roller, might as well have a little siesta while these blankets dry, and then ease on home." He looked at the trail leading up the headwall ridge, seeing the trip back across the big meadow, across the far side of the mountain toward home, and sighed. Roller shook his massive

Some horses seem to have a lot of attitude. Truth is, they all do, but most are too wily to let on. This big bay stud is laughing at the mares at the Pitchfork Ranch in West Texas. Photo © Bob Moorhouse

blankets, the split reins tangling around his feet. Easy enough for him to tip over and drown. Merv could only stand helplessly on the shore, watching, "Goddammit, Roller...," he cursed—or perhaps it was closer to prayer.

The colt's eyes showed white. He snorted and coughed, kicked and kicked at the hobbles. Finally, somehow, he broke free. Still hauling the heavy blankets and soaking-wet saddle, he lunged through the hidden underwater boulders toward shore. Power doubled, he clawed his way back up through the rocks until with one final desperate heave, he stood, dripping and quivering on the grass.

Merv reached out slowly, took the reins, eased off

shoulders like a dog, and sighed too. He dropped his head to the grass. He was hungry.

The sun has left Peggy's lawn, and the children are inside playing a game on the living room rug. She takes one deep breath as she sees Merv and the big bay colt emerge from the rocky canyon that leads to the high country, all in shadow now. She stubs out the last cigarette, pours out her cold coffee and starts to knead the dough down into rolls for Merv's dinner.

Merv shakes his head as he finishes the story of his day. "That old Roller. I thought I was gonna lose him, by God. By God, colt's got some heart to him, don't he?"

*A flock of sheep enjoys the Spring grass in California's
Mother Lode country. Photo © Carolyn Fox*

"You don't quite let yourself believe that it all is yours. Does this belong to me, you might wonder. Yet you know that you can only manage it and nurture it for all the things that make it grow. Microbes and worms, snails and skunks, snakes and frogs, and grasses flowering in the Spring. They do the job and you call it yours, but you don't quite believe it. Does it really belong to you? It must be a difficult question for God."

TIM FINDLEY, 2005

Spring paints the foothills of California's Tehachapi Range in the southern San Joaquin Valley with blooming lupines. Photo © Larry Angier. Below: Cows serenely graze the southern Sierra Nevada hills near Springville, California as they have for centuries. Where they roam, wildlife abounds and carpets of flowers cloak the hills in Spring. Photo © Carolyn Fox

Twenty bucks and a brush with greatness

PAINTINGS BY CRAIG SHEPPARD. ART AND WORDS © SOPHIE SHEPPARD.

After my mother's death, I began the task of dismantling the house in Reno that had been her home for more than fifty years. Deep in a drawer in the studio she had shared with my father, I found a felt armband. To the black elastic strap is attached a palm-sized red circle, stitched all around. Appliquéd to the center are two-inch-high blue felt numbers: 106. A large button is pinned to the bottom of the red felt circle. It reads:

> *World Series Rodeo Contestant*
> *106*
> *Madison Square Garden - 1934*

The armband belonged to my father. His stories of himself as a cowboy—the Oklahoma kid with the ears that stuck out from his otherwise Greek-god head, arriving young and green in New York City to ride the bulls, packing his saddle over his shoulder—figured large in our family's mythology. While he told them, he rubbed our backs as if to knead his words deep into our skin. We loved his Oklahoma drawl, the stories of himself, his dad and the wild, wild West, before life had been tamed, scaled down to the postwar tract houses of Reno, the teaching job at the University, and the washing machine in the kitchen that my mother made me sit on each spin cycle to keep the dishes from rattling out of the cupboards.

It took my father eight long years to make it

through college. He cowboyed and rode the rodeo circuit between semesters, perhaps to belie the label of "sissy" that he feared because he studied painting. When he left Oklahoma to ride the bulls at Madison Square Garden, he pried up the insole in the heel of his right cowboy boot, inserted a brand new twenty-dollar bill, pushed the insole back into place and put his boot back on, secure that he would have the bus fare home.

The inevitable happened. Broke and ready to leave the city, he sat down on the edge of the saggy mattress in his rented room and pulled off his boot. Reaching down inside the fancy stitched and appliquéd boot top, he peeled up the insole to retrieve his emergency money. But what he found, what he pulled out of that boot, was a tattered piece of limp green lace, tacky with glue and damp with sweat rather than the crisp new twenty that had crackled when he had folded it up to save it there weeks before.

Clutching the limp green rag, my father packed his saddle across town and up the steps to the U.S. Mint. He walked up to one of the windows at the front counter. As he bent to lay his saddle down, latigos slapped on the polished marble floor. One stirrup slipped to bang an echo through the lobby. Pushing that ragged little piece of green slowly through the window toward the teller, he said in his Oklahoma drawl, "This used to be a twenty-dollar bill."

The teller had no doubts. She had seen his saddle. She saw his blond good looks and the ears that stood out from his head like handles on a jug. She slipped that damp green lace in across the counter with her right hand and with her left, she sent him the brand-new twenty that would return him to Oklahoma, no questions asked.

My father taught me to ride. I realize now how much of his buckaroo pride he swallowed to ride those stable nags with me on the streets in the outskirts of Reno. And we loved it when he emerged from the house on a Saturday morning with his lasso. He'd holler at us, "Run by and beller like a calf." When we did, his loop would snare us and we'd fall down on the green lawn, engulfed in tangles of rope and hysterical laughter.

When I was nine, my father was awarded a Fulbright and our family moved to Norway. My father and mother set up their household and studios on the island of Ørmoya near Oslo. The north country light was good for his painting but the winter days were too brief. Norwegian afternoons stretched out long and unproductive until he unpacked his Japanese sumi brushes and India ink. I remember him sitting in the fading daylight surrounded by a sea of white paper covered with calligraphic brushstrokes. Not oriental ideograms, but images of horses. Galloping, bucking, rearing and snorting. Stallions, mares and colts. He aimed to distill the image of a horse out of the fewest lines possible. Sometimes he made fifty drawings an evening. Out of that he would choose two or three, culling the rest. The ones he kept ran with an easy line like a fluid jazz riff, his personal song that all was well, that hope still ran free in the world.—*Sophie Sheppard*

Craig Sheppard was born in 1913 in Lawton, Oklahoma. He grew up learning to buckaroo from his father and was encouraged to paint by his mother. Sheppard studied art at the University of Oklahoma in Norman, and throughout his college years toured the professional rodeo circuit riding saddle broncs and bulls, eventually bull riding in Madison Square Garden. With his wife, the noted sculptor Yolande Jacobson, Sheppard moved to Nevada in 1947 to develop the Art Department for the University of Nevada in Reno. A Fulbright to Norway in 1956, a sabbatical to France in 1961 and another to Mexico in 1969 established his reputation internationally. Sheppard's work has been published, exhibited, documented and collected throughout the western United States and Europe, from the Nevada Museum of Art to the Museum of Modern Art in Paris. The Nevada State Journal has described Sheppard as, "probably the most important visual artist dealing in Nevada themes…a unique combination of the sophisticated academician and the salty pioneer prospector."

Craig Sheppard's first portfolio, "Western Drawings in Brush and Ink," was published in 1980 by the University of Nevada Press, two years after his death. Twenty years later, his daughter, painter and writer Sophie Sheppard, honored her father's memory with a selection of her favorite drawings in a portfolio called "The Year of the Horse," Carmel Publishing, 2002. Practically the entire inventory of "The Year of the Horse" was destroyed in a flash flood in Surprise Valley two years later.

The life and times of Charlie Russell

"Loops And Swift Horses Are Surer Than Lead,"
oil 29-1/2"x47-1/2", 1916.

Charlie Russell's friend Wallace Coburn told about a time when Coburn was riding for the Circle C outfit. The nighthawk came into camp to report forty horses missing. Foreman William Jaycox scrambled into his clothes and rode to the top of a hill where he saw the horses racing toward camp, being chased by a bear. The bear swiped the tail of Charlie Shufelt's horse, which bucked and shied. Joe Reynolds finally got a loop over the bear's back feet. Frank Howe dropped a loop over her head. The horses had to hold the bear while the men killed her with rocks. In the early morning they were half-dressed and hadn't brought their guns.

In painting the scene, Charlie Russell gave Frank Howe proper clothes and a gun, but the title tells the real story.

Lady Bronc Rider, ca. 1925.
C.M. Russell Museum,
Great Falls, Montana.

Charlie Russell was a frequent letter writer who filled his letters with drawings and watercolor sketches. Done with Russell's skilled hand, they also show his wit, humor and ability to capture a fleeting moment.

Undaunted spirit, undying love

© LARRY TURNER.

The bed and dresser remain. The screened porch, tattered and weathered, speaks of near-perfect summer evenings over half a century ago. Eighty-nine-year-old Herman Vowell sits near the venerable copper-clad Malleable range, remembering.

On Valentine's Day, 1948, her birthday, Betty told Herman that she might be pregnant. "I think we have our little one growing inside," she had whispered affectionately to her buckaroo husband.

Herman (foreman), his brother Ray and Betty managed W.C. Dalton's Steele Swamp Pitchfork Ranch in the remote Devil's Garden of extreme northeast California.

Herman came to the Swamp as a lean rawhide buckaroo in 1936. That first evening, he walked up to the rimrock and watched the sun set over the valley, distant mountains and nearby juniper and pine hillsides. His spirit soared. "My heart belongs here," he said to himself. To this day his spirit dances when the Swamp comes into view.

Herman met his pretty bride at a California ranch in 1938. He had been sent to round up steers that Dalton pastured there. "My heart skipped a few beats when I first saw Betty. She must've thought that I had a speech impediment because I could not get a word out edgeways, let alone straight, when we were introduced."

Betty was the queen of the Madrone Rodeo. Herman entered the bronc riding event and won before 4,000 cheering fans, but the fan he wanted to most impress was Betty. Herman and Betty were

Betty loved the ranch and its isolation, the simple life and, most of all, her sweet cowboy.
Photo © Herman Vowell

married in 1942.

On March 27, 1948, eighteen inches of snow fell at the Swamp. At breakfast the next morning, Herman noticed Betty stopping to hold her side so he kept an eye on the ranch house as the team of Belgians pulled the wagon while he and Ray forked hay to the cattle.

"God must have turned my head from pitching hay at that moment that day," Herman says. He saw Betty open the kitchen door and frantically wave a dishtowel.

Ray took over the team. Herman ran to the house where he found her unconscious on the kitchen floor. He carefully placed her in their bed, then rushed to the phone, hoping that the huge snowstorm had not cut off their service—a rather primitive fifty miles of telephone line strung between juniper trees from the Swamp to Alturas, Modoc County's seat.

In Alturas, operator Rita Smerl answered. "Rita, Betty is in bad shape," Herman said. "We need a doctor out here badly."

"I'll do my best, Herman," Rita replied, "but with the storm the road may not be open for days, or even weeks. We'll get help your way as soon as we can."

Nearest neighbor Thelma Archer, wife of the Willow Creek Ranch manager, overheard the party-line conversation. She saddled up, left a note for her husband, and rode toward Steele Swamp, twenty miles distant.

Rita reached Herman's cowboy friend Mervin

Herman Vowell finds joy in remembering the happy years with "that pretty lady filly of mine." They were champion team ropers and won buckles together as rodeo riders.
Photo © Larry Turner

Wilde who had recently taken over as head of Klamath County's Search and Rescue in Malin, Oregon, fifty miles by road northwest of Steele Swamp. Dr. Jack Martin from Topeka, Kansas, had set up a practice in Malin just three weeks earlier. Mervin convinced Jack of Betty's grave condition and arranged a flight with pilot Bud Arnold in his Piper Cub.

Jack quickly gathered his medical supplies, including extra plasma, and headed to Malin's tiny dirt-runway airport. Bud ran his plane up and down the runway for forty-five minutes, packing it enough to try a takeoff. "Okay Doc, we have one shot at this to clear the fence. You're going to have to help by pushing the plane and jumping in at the last moment." Without hesitation the young doctor hopped onto one of the plane's skis, hoisting himself into the door as the plane cleared the fence by two inches.

Fifteen minutes later they arrived at the Swamp, landing perfectly on a makeshift runway marked with gunnysacks in the level pasture near the barn. The day before, the field had been a quagmire of mud. Herman says the fresh snow and cold was "a godsend, allowing them to land."

Luckily, the plane had its 65hp engine replaced with a 95hp engine the day before. "If it wasn't for that," Bud says, "we wouldn't have cleared the fence."

Jack diagnosed Betty with a ruptured ectopic pregnancy with internal bleeding. Her survival depended on immediate surgery, but it was beyond his training. He called a fellow Kansas surgeon, Raymond Tice, in Klamath Falls, seventy miles distant. Bud flew to Klamath Falls, picking up Raymond, who had secured a hundred pounds of sterile surgical equipment from Hillside Hospital. Within an hour, they were at Steele Swamp.

In the meantime, the Vowell brothers and Jack

Herman proposed to Betty the day before Pearl Harbor was bombed on December 7, 1941. She agreed, and they honeymooned in a cow camp. Photo courtesy Herman Vowell

Martin made a makeshift operating table in the kitchen. Two sawhorses held a kitchen door and a mattress. The stove was stoked with wood. Water was boiling.

Working quickly, Raymond arranged his surgical instruments on the kitchen counter. Betty was placed on the mattress table. A chunk of firewood elevated her legs. All the light was mustered, including kerosene lanterns and two generator-charged kitchen bulbs. Jack administered anesthesia. Later, brother Ray held a flashlight to illuminate Doc Raymond's stitching.

The procedure was straightforward but risky—an incision opening the abdomen to stop the bleeding and remove the damaged tube, closing the incision and administering blood and plasma to help arrest the surgical shock. The doctors were worried the patient was not strong enough to survive the surgery and, in view of the operating conditions, the risk of a deadly infection.

Herman prayed that his beloved's life would be spared. He proposed to Betty on December 6, 1941, the day before Pearl Harbor was bombed. They were parked on a hill overlooking the ocean at Santa Cruz, California. It was their first kiss. Later that evening he asked Betty's parents for permission to marry.

Their first honeymoon night at the Swamp was spent in the Weed Valley cow camp buckaroo cabin. The other buckaroos set up their tents a good distance away, giving the newlyweds the "honeymoon suite."

Herman thought about picnics by horseback from the ranch house to the distant hills. The smell of sage and juniper mixed with the fresh high desert air and the perspiration coming off the horses. Betty loved the ranch, the isolation, the critters and wildlife, the simple life. Herman would surprise her with fresh wildflowers. She would giggle, nuzzle into him and say, "Thank you my sweet cowboy. I love you."

The old cabin has little furniture now but it is crowded with memories for Herman. Photo © Larry Turner

The early Spring sun had set when Ray came into the room and said, "Herman, the doctors are done and she's doing fine. I'll go do the chores."

The weight of the world fell from Herman's chest as he wiped the tears away, thanking God, the doctors, Bud and Ray for the great news. He kissed Betty gently on the forehead. "How is she?" he asked Raymond.

"She will be fine," the surgeon said.

Brother Ray paused in his chores, staring into the clear, cold night, thanking the powers that be for allowing his cherished sister-in-law to live.

Thelma arrived after her long horse ride, exhausted but buoyant after hearing about the operation's success. The operating room was turned back into a kitchen as she made a hearty supper of ham, eggs, bacon and biscuits.

A Forest Service vehicle arrived after an all-day drive on the treacherous roads and took Dr. Raymond Tice back to town. Jack spent the night attending Betty, departing with Bud in the morning. Bud

would fly a nurse in later in the day.

Betty's story made headlines around the country. Spring brought back the sandhill cranes and a bellowing new calf crop. Betty healed. The love between Betty and Herman became stronger than ever. They adopted a daughter, Susie.

They spent twelve more years at Steele Swamp. No one has lived full-time at the Swamp since.

"It was heaven. No one was happier than we were—thanks to the courageous people who came to our aid that fateful day," says Herman. "The spirit of these people will live in me forever."

Herman, Betty and Ray eventually purchased a small ranch in Malin so Susie could attend school. Betty died of cancer in 1966 at age forty-five. Bud Arnold succumbed to a heart attack in 1953. Ray Vowell passed away in 1999 and Jack Martin in 2004. Raymond Tice and Herman continue to maintain their friendship with visits and telephone conversations. "We're forever linked by that pretty lady filly of mine. God rest her soul. I love her."

Jack Swanson

When it comes to portraying the California buckaroo, no one has better credentials than Jack Swanson. In addition to being a man of great artistic talent, Jack roped, rode and wrangled with the last of the great vaqueros in the Tehachapi Mountains half a century ago. Later, he worked with buckaroos in Oregon, breaking and selling wild horses. Many of Jack's paintings include the distinctive California oaks and tawny coastal hills that surround his studio/ranch. As for horses, he raises them, trains them

"Riders of the San Joaquin," oil, 40"x70". The beautiful grassland in the foothills of the Sierra dries up in late spring. Cowboys gather the livestock and move them into the high Sierra.

"Trailing the Cattle," oil, 40"x70".
These are good vaqueros, many descended from the early cattlemen who worked for Miller and Lux, Tejon and other large, early California ranches. Their traditional trappings include slick fork saddles, tapaderos and rawhide reatas. The cattle are of the horned breed used in the heyday of the vaquero.

and brings them into his in-studio stall for the kind of intimacy no camera can provide.

Jack Swanson's paintings have hung in the White House and are in the permanent collections of the National Cowboy & Western Heritage Museum, Oklahoma City, Oklahoma and the Cowboy Artists of America Museum, Kerrville, Texas.

"*The emancipation of women may have begun not with the vote, nor in the cities where women marched and carried signs and protested, but rather when they mounted a good cow horse and realized how different and fine the view.*"

FOLK HISTORIAN JOYCE GIBSON ROACH,
"THE COWGIRLS"
CORDOVAN PUBLISHING, 1977

DaeNel Douglas, buckaroo at the Roaring Springs Ranch, Frenchglen, Oregon.
Photo © Larry Turner

Hattie Feazelle has been leading the Fiesta Days Parade in Santa Barbara, California, since it began eighty-one years ago. In 2005 she was honored as "La Reina del Fiesta" (queen of the fiesta). At ninety-four, Hattie rides her paint horse that she renamed Chibita (little goat) after he ate her straw hat. An active member of several riding groups, she also puts up about two hundred jars of delicious jam every year to give friends at Christmas.
Photo © Heather Hafleigh

Jeff McKenzie leads his daughter Katherine Rose horseback outside their Plush, Oregon, ranch. Hart Mountain looms in the background.
Photo © Larry Turner

*Pete French crew at chuck wagon, probably early 1900s.
Charles (Chuck) Goodnight fitted out an army wagon to
become the cook wagon/larder for his crews on the
Goodnight-Loving Cattle Trail in the 1860s. The "chuck"
wagon is a living monument to Goodnight's ingenuity.
Photograph by R.W. Heck. Photo © Tom Robinson*

"*I had rather be shut up in a very modest cottage, with my books, my family and a few old friends, dining on simple bacon, and letting the world roll on as it liked than to occupy the most splendid post which any human power can give.*"

THOMAS JEFFERSON, 1788

Clay Peterson and his son Luke are roasting their hot dogs while waiting for the beans to warm up. The Peterson family has a long heritage of taking pack trips each Sunday during the Summer season. This gives them a well-deserved break from the hard work at their cattle ranch in Jackson, Montana. Photo © Cynthia Baldauf

Texas roundup

PHOTOS © BOB MOORHOUSE

Pitchfork Land and Cattle Company has survived almost a century-and-a-quarter of droughts and depressed cattle markets. Today, it is bigger than ever and uses computers and helicopters, but a cowboy from the original ranch owned by the Williams family in 1883 would still feel right at home.

Every Spring and Fall, cowboys round up and cull around 5,000 mother cows over 165,000 acres of dry, rugged land. A cowboy might ride fifteen miles in a single pasture, gathering the "South Texas-cross cows" that have adapted to the tough country. Riders are mounted on the good horses for which the Pitchfork is famed, especially the "Pitchfork Gray," a gray with black mane and tail. In the 125-horse remuda, each cowboy has his own string—chosen by him from the two-year-olds. They are his to keep as long as he rides for the Pitchfork. During the gathers, a cowboy changes horses several times a day to let his tired mounts rest.

Out on the range, meals are served from a chuck wagon. There might be fancier rolling kitchens, but none accommodate the country so well. Quarters are a bedroll and teepee.

The Pitchfork stays true to the tradition and ethic that has allowed it to thrive and grow. Ranch manager Bob Moorhouse has been with the Pitchfork for thirty-four years, starting as an assistant manager. The Williams family still owns the Pitchfork and the cowboys still eat at the table that was used in 1883.

"The owners like tradition," Bob Moorhouse says. "And cowboys like tradition. Everybody should."

David Ross shakes out a loop as the horses in the Pitchfork Ranch remuda wait for the morning selection. Photo © Bob Moorhouse

Tim Stout uses windmill-drawn water for an early wash, but you'd have to be "pretty tough or pretty thirsty" to drink most of the Pitchfork water.
Photo © Bob Moorhouse

73

Above: Dick Sayers is building a loop to practice heeling while driving the cattle. Pasture by pasture, Pitchfork cattle are rounded up across land that is "hard as hell to work."
Left: The cowboys wait for the cow boss's orders. It's all teamwork, men and horses gathering and moving cattle.
Photos © Bob Moorhouse

Left: Doug Harney loads bedrolls and makes sure everything is secure. Below: James Gholson drives the wagon during Spring works. Wherever the cowboys camp, the wagons and remuda will be there, too. Photo © Bob Moorhouse

*During Spring branding Chad Braker enjoys putting his traditional skills to practical use. After the cowboys get the cattle in the pen, it's time for roping, riding, branding, doctoring, tagging and castrating.
Photo © Bob Moorhouse*

*Dick Sayers and Travis Hale show that it's all in the timing.
Photo © Bob Moorhouse*

David Ross puts the Pitchfork "stamp" on one, while Chris Abbott holds the calf down. Photo © Bob Moorhouse

Dick Sayers and Chad Braker have a little fun. The cow may be stubborn and ornery, but the cowboys will triumph— no matter how many it takes! Photo © Bob Moorhouse

Clay Timmons drags one to the fire. Photo © Bob Moorhouse

Chris Abbott and Ross Ericsson drink out of Pitchfork china. Photo © Bob Moorhouse

Fred Fine, born March 15, 1880, is draped over a chair with his hat cocked and his feet up on photographer John McMullen's "fence." Picture taken around 1900 shows Fred as a young buckaroo, all slicked up to impress the ladies in town. Photo © Tom Robinson

Mick Goettle has been cowboying all his life. He and his wife Earlene live and work at the Stucky Ranch in the quietly beautiful Nevada Creek valley near Avon, Montana, where lush, gravity irrigated grasslands produce hay for Winter feeding and surrounding mountain pasture provides Summer grazing. Photo © Charles W. Guildner

Cowboys, horses and dogs

BY JOEL NELSON © 1987

A ship has her sails and a rudder
To help her in crossing the seas
The writer has pencil and paper
And old men have arthritic knees.

The rich man has money, the poor man has hope,
The gardener has seed catalogs,
And cowboys have horses and dogs, my friend,
Cowboys have horses and dogs.

The horse is the cowboy's partner
And the better half of the two
'Cause he packs the load and does more'n his share
In all of the cow work they do.

And the ol' dog's his pal through sun and snow
Through the dust and through the bogs.
So cowboys have horses and dogs for friends
Cowboys, horses and dogs.

And sometimes a lady comes ridin' along
Seems to fit right in with the scheme
'Cause the cowboys, horses, and dogs and her
Seem to dream the same kinda dream.

She can dress up and shine and the touch of her lips
Could turn men into princes from frogs,
But she'd rather be where the air's clean and free
With her cowboys, horses and dogs,
'Cause she loves her cowboys, horses and dogs.

An Autumn gather started in morning fog, Bonham Ranch, Horse Creek, Wyoming. Riders headed in several directions to round up more than 1,500 cattle. Photo © Mary Steinbacher

The Wager kids are ranch hands taking care of livestock on land that has belonged to their mother's family since 1887 when the Jicarilla Apache Reservation was established. Dad, Lakota Sioux Rome Wager, is a cowboy, champion rodeo rider, Hollywood stuntman, horse trainer, evangelical preacher and a direct descendant of the Lakota warriors who defeated Custer at the Little Bighorn. Back row: Rome, Jr., sixteen; Cheyenne, ten; Gary, nineteen, and Casey, fifteen. Front row: Six-year-old triplets Justin Other, Jesse James and Charmayne. Photo © Gene Peach

82

"In this place there is a mountain called the Sierra Chusque or mountain of agriculture from which (when it rains) the water flows in abundance creating large sand bars on which the Navajos plant their corn: it is a fine country for stock or agriculture. There is another mountain called the Mesa Calabasa where these beads we wear on our necks have been handed down from generation to generation and where we were told by our forefathers never to leave our own country."

CHIEF BARBONCITO NEGOTIATING THE NAVAJO TREATY WITH GENERAL W.T. SHERMAN.
THE NAVAJO WOULD BE RETURNED TO THEIR ANCESTRAL LANDS FROM FORCED EXILE
AT BOSQUE REDONDO IN EASTERN NEW MEXICO IN 1868.

Patronizing, paternalistic attitudes put Indians into boarding schools where they were forbidden to speak their own language. This group at the Fort McDermitt Shoshone-Paiute reservation in Nevada's Black Rock Desert have obviously been encouraged to frolic on the lawn with baseball bats and badminton racquets, overseen by a Native sheriff (ca. 1915). Photographer R.W. Heck. Photo © Tom Robinson

By the time John Muir first saw the San Joaquin Valley, sheep had been grazing it for over one hundred years, numbering over three hundred thousand in the valley in 1833. Yet, thirty-five years later in 1868, Muir describes this sheep-ravaged valley as "the floweriest piece of world I ever walked."

JOHN MUIR,
LETTER TO MRS. EZRA CARR,
JULY 19, 1868

"Sheep Mountain," Pine Forest range, northwest Nevada, home to the Dufurrena Sheep and Cattle Company.
Photo © Linda Dufurrena

"Faintly, borne up and muted with the whir of wind through the pines, came the sound of bells and bleating. It was a sheep camp. I filled my lungs and yelled, and in a little while my father answered. I came cupping down through the canyons in a call as old as the first Basque mountain man. It was my father's sheep camp."

ROBERT LAXALT, "SWEET PROMISED LAND," UNIVERSITY OF NEVADA PRESS, 1957

Hay crew luncheon

© CAROLYN DUFURRENA. ILLUSTRATION © JOHN BARDWELL.

It's twenty years ago now. Tim and his brothers were just starting out; we had a year's lease on 800 head of cows and a bunch of flood-irrigated alfalfa near the edge of the Black Rock Desert. I had a garden out my back door. It grew just fine as long as you planted right on the wet edge of the ditches, but closed up tighter than Fort Knox between waterings.

We'd spent the first three years of our married life in West Texas, in the city, and this was the bargain. After three, we'd take the nest egg we'd made in the booming oil fields of West Texas; we'd come home and build the ranch with Tim's brothers. So this was my rookie year as a rancher's wife and certainly as a ranch cook.

It was first crop and I was feeding the hay crew. Not that I didn't have experience entertaining, I thought as I paged through my cookbooks. I had a trunk full of journals from Auntie Gertrude, detailing years of Chicago bridge luncheons and brunches, each entry embellished with notes the following day, and all ending with the words, "a great success!"

I knew how to fold a napkin, how to decora-tively peel a cucumber. Of course I could feed people.

"We'll be in at noon," Tim threw over his shoulder, on his way out that morning. "Stacking crew'll be here, so there'll be six or seven of us."

The June sun ripened as I considered the menu. My young son and I gardened, gathering lettuce, the last of the peas. Ah, I thought, wiping the perspiration from my eyes, a summer soup would be just the thing.

When the men came in to wash, the table was all set, dishes sparkling, napkins folded attractively. Each place had a lovely, garnished bowl of smooth green soup; a single quiche Lorraine was daintily sliced in the table's center. There'd be one piece left over, I was thinking. I'd counted.

Pleasantries exchanged, Ray, the contract harrowed operator, sat first. Six-four, he's a broad-shouldered Basco who ate at ranch tables all over the county; I knew the report of my first Summer luncheon would spread quickly throughout the land.

"This soup's cold!" he exploded.

"Of course!" I replied.

"What the hell's in it?" he fired back.

He looked incredulously at the smooth green surface, the basil leaves thoughtfully garnishing the center, no doubt suspecting pond algae or moss from the trough.

"It's Potage St. Germain! It's a puree of Spring peas and lettuce. It's supposed to be cold!" I explained, sure that I would inject some class into this worthy but provincial group. Tim's two brothers and the three field hands ducked their heads to hide their faces, and ate. It didn't take long.

Someone reached for a slice of quiche. "Got any ketchup?"

I was horrified. What about the delicate bouquet of herbs and spices?

Tim gave me The Look, however, and I thought, oh fine, and went to the fridge, visualizing the line under Auntie Gertrude's luncheon entry evaporate: "A great success" indeed.

Then true disaster struck. "Where's the meat?" Tim asked quietly as, miffed at the ketchup issue, I moved things around in the refrigerator.

"Meat? This is a summer luncheon," I replied.

His response was to start digging in the freezer for pork chops. It had taken the men about thirty seconds to inhale the lovely quiche triangles, and they were looking at me expectantly. I was stumped.

Tim fried some meat and reheated potatoes while I salved my dignity, and the men somehow finished their meal. I never heard the stories that must have made the rounds that Summer with the hay crew, but I'm sure I was temporarily famous.

I was really glad later on when we got to be cowboys. Tim was never totally comfortable on a baler anyway, and he took over instruction as I learned to make stew and sourdough biscuits, and great pots of beans to haul up to brandings.

I heard the stories of cooks however. Quinn River had been a stopping place at mealtime for more than a century; the big railroad bell out back

ringing at six, twelve and six to call whoever was near the headquarters to come and eat. The usual twenty places were set at the table, three times a day, plus whoever showed up. People would time their arrivals for 11:45—well, there was nothing else out there for seventy miles.

I asked my father-in-law, who ran that ranch for twenty years, about the cooks. "Who was the best?" Tim said he'd never tell me, and he didn't. "Had a lot of good cooks," he said. "Damn good cooks, and easy to get along with. You knew they were good cooks because lots of people stopped to eat.

"They all had their strong points," he added diplomatically. My husband said, "Well." Names were not named, but it became clearer to me why he didn't get all excited when I suggested hotcakes in the morning.

"Just can't eat breakfast," Tim would say, looking sideways at the fried eggs and hotcakes. Still feeling the hotcakes of his seventeenth summer, the ones that soaked up entire bottles of syrup, swelled in his belly until afternoon, expanding with a quality that the World Health Organization would do well to learn about, for one of those cakes would have fed a starving family of four for a week.

That life had changed by the time we had come back from Texas. The big ranches around there didn't run a cookhouse any more; there was just me, and my quiche recipe. I have learned to fill in the gaps.

All my soups are hot now. When there's a crew to feed, my menus revolve around meat and potatoes. There are no delicate blends of herbs and spices, unless I'm cooking for my own friends. The boys are just hungry, and they'll finish pretty much whatever you put in front of them and hope there's plenty, then politely thank the cook.

Still, every once in a while, I can't resist putting a soft-boiled egg down in front of a cowboy—in an egg cup.

Spanish Ranch, Nevada, 2000. Stan Jones waits for the remuda to settle as sunlight breaks over the desert horizon. Photo © Adam Jahiel

Solitude Words and Photos © Adam Jahiel

The space and solitude of the cow camps in the Great Basin, northern Nevada in particular, have latched onto my soul like little else ever has. What I thought would be a quick foray in and out of an unknown world that I was curious about, became first an interest, then a passion, and finally a necessity.

I live in an area most would consider remote and unpopulated. People look at me in a strange way when I tell them that I'm going to the desert cow camps to clear the winter cobwebs out of my head. But every Spring, after the excitement and novelty of Winter begin to rub off, I get the itch to head to the Great Basin, where my personal

Horse shadows. Each buckaroo has a string of half a dozen horses that travel with him during gathers. Each horse has different talents and uses. Sometimes when the work is particularly hard, several horses will be used in a day. Photo © Adam Jahiel

yearly renewal takes place.

As I drive west through the Salt Lake desert, I begin to take leave of my self-absorbed condition and give myself over to the land, sky and clouds. My sense of scale in relation to the natural world around me ratchets down to a realistic level where I am a tiny particle, part of a much larger world, as insignificant as anything could possibly be, a pair of eyes and ears, taking in a mite's view of the world I am just passing through.

I drive on. As road after road becomes narrower, rougher, I am rewarded by the feeling that home is just a dot of ink on some map. My

Three Horses of the Apocalypse, Homedale Idaho, 1993. In a cloud of dust and hoofbeats, Martin Black works three horses which are still a bit on the wild side. Photo © Adam Jahiel

Spanish Ranch, Nevada, 1995. Anthony Gonzales holds onto his haltered horse, which he will use to wrangle the cow camp's remuda the next morning. Photo © Adam Jahiel

"*The horse...the only animal that can match reflexes with the cat,
endure longer than the wolf, run faster than the deer.*"

KUWAITI SAYING

world is here, sandwiched between the brown clouds of dust that my tires are making, and the huge, black and white shifting clouds that hover overhead. Like the song says, I can see for miles and miles and miles. As I look north, I know the mountains in the background belong to another state. Here, political boundaries seem artificial, manmade, nonsensical.

As I sight a cow camp in the distance, I feel at once the relief of not being completely lost, and the anticipation of who and what lies ahead. After years of visits, I know that something here will be familiar, whether cowboy, cook, horse, camp, or, at the very least,

With evening approaching and the IL Ranch cowboys' teepees in the background, a lone metal chair, one of the cow camp's luxuries, waits for someone to relax in it for a while before turning in for the day.
Photo © Adam Jahiel

Roping a Cloud, IL Ranch, Nevada, 1994.
Mark Jones throws a loop at daybreak as he catches horses for the cowboys for that day's work. Photo © Adam Jahiel

93

something completely new, something I am both accustomed to and revel in.

I'm comfortable here, in my own element. I will be judged, if at all, on very basic terms. Once, as I pulled up to a camp full of unfamiliar faces, I was approached by a handful of cowboys. Their spokesman looked at me for a moment and asked, "Do you have a fishing pole with you?"

I have grown to love and admire these friends, old and new. Despite all the hardships and uncertainty of what their lives entail, I will always be in awe and envious of all that they do and represent. I feel more like myself here than anywhere else in the world.

In a Quonset hut, the only building that might be considered habitable at Winter's Camp, an empty bunk and chair sit silently waiting for their next visitor. Photo © Adam Jahiel

*John Adamson watches as Doug Groves ropes horses
for the buckaroos at the TS Ranch, Battle Mountain,
Nevada. Photo © Adam Jahiel*

So spring can come

WORDS AND PHOTOS © STEVEN H. RICH.

Some things are so beautiful you have to share them. After five years of searing, gut-wrenching, heartbreaking drought, the snows had come, and then the rains. My brother John called on his cell phone, from horseback. He said there were thousands of acres of wildflowers and tall grass where there had been bare, dusty ground. There were seedlings everywhere.

"Native grass is just exploding! Get here as soon as you can," John said, with joy in his voice. "It'll do you good."

John knows how I feel about this land. He feels

the same way. He also knows we made the down payment for this ranch from my wife Melinda's small trust fund.

When Melinda was fourteen years old, her parents had caught an early flight from Mexico so her surgeon father could save a child's leg. The airliner hit a mountain near Las Vegas. Their five orphaned daughters didn't get much in the settlement. The down payment was most of what was left of Melinda's share.

Melinda loved me. She loved my Dad (whose idea it was to buy the ranch) and my rancher family. Melinda wept when she signed the check. There weren't 500 pounds of grass on the

This area was burned by the Bureau of Land Management and reseeded by the Rich family. Forage for cattle and wildlife include globe mallow, western wheatgrass, needle and thread, bottlebrush, squirreltail, crested wheatgrass and Indian ricegrass. Shrubs include big sage, four-wing saltbush, and yucca. Trees are pinion and juniper with ponderosa pine on mountaintops. Photo © Steven H. Rich

Yucca blooms on deep soil, rocky soil in deserts, grasslands and open woods. Its fruit and flowers have been used as food for centuries.
Photo © Steven H. Rich

whole place. We rested and rested our new ranch. I really believed the professors who told me that "rest"—no grazing—would bring back the native biodiversity.

I watched with great anticipation only to see the same pitiful response year after year. In wet years, some of our millions of sagebrush plants did manage to grow a little seed. A little tansy mustard and a few other annuals would grow at the base of some sagebrush. In dry years—no sage seed, no mustard. Sometimes a little of the sagebrush died.

Twenty years earlier, immediately across our east fence, the Forest Service had root-plowed a wide, miles-long swath of dense, grass-choking sage and drilled in a seed mix. That Forest Service land produced millions of pounds of native and introduced seeds, some of which washed and blew over on our side. They also produced a mighty bio-mass of wildlife and beef.

None of those seeds ever germinated on our side of the fence. I'm pretty sure the harvester ants got them all. We produced lots of harvester ants.

After several years I gave in and started planting seeds with equipment. We bought some seed and harvested native seed. We spent a lot of money. I was so aware of those costs that I wouldn't spend money on a new suit to wear to church for twenty years. Mom finally bought me one for Dad's funeral. I have very kind feelings toward the Natural Resources Conservation Service, Bureau of Land Management and Forest Service folks who trusted and worked with us, even using range fire as a tool. The whole family helped. We'd come in every night from planting with our faces black with dirt and ashes, our eyes red and stinging, hopeful of rain.

The seeds grew. Wildlife moved in. Their activities—dung, urine, hoofprints—and those of the cows in the brush surrounding the seedings, grew more grass between the sage than we did with our work. It was great not being left out of springtime. We grew thousands of acres of grass and volunteer wildflowers.

I asked my Dad why he chose that barren, brush-infested, hopeless ranch.

"I had my reasons," he said. "One of them was you. Look how hard you've worked. Think how much you've learned."

It was that sort of hell-for-leather logic that caused us to affectionately refer to Dad (John P. Rich Sr.) as Mad Baggins.

"One of my other reasons was that I just couldn't stand to watch it die," he said. Then he grinned. "I knew if Melinda's money was in it you'd make it work."

Dad leveraged that reasoning with his grandchildren. They hauled water, fixed fence and herded cows for miles on foot with their granddad, who called them his Can-Do-Kids. For much of that time he was filled with cancer and pain. Our children and their cousins are as close as brothers

Roaming livestock have prepared the soil and trimmed the grasses so flowers and forage, including prickly pear cactus, can thrive together providing a banquet for deer, birds, rabbits and other small creatures. Photo © Steven H. Rich

and sisters. Every one of them is someone you'd be proud to know.

Right after Pearl Harbor, Dad joined the Marines. He passed up officers' training to stick with his Carlson's Raiders demolition squad in hopes of blowing stuff up behind enemy lines. In his mind, placing me under a debt of honor was a compliment. He loved to see our planted pastures wave in the wind and watch the wildlife there. I loved being with him. He always backed me up. Mom backed us all up.

Dad told me the day before he died that for more than a week he'd seen the guys in his next-world Marine escort waiting for him. Over a thousand people attended his funeral.

A few years later, the worst drought in recorded history hit our Arizona country. Most of the grass we had planted died. Native species did bet-

ter than the introduced ones (we had only planted noninvasives), but the natives died too, in the millions. Mice, voles, lizards, ground squirrels, rabbits, coyotes, birds, deer and other wildlife died. Large areas of sagebrush, juniper and piñon trees died.

We cut our cattle herd way back. Then we sent the cows away and sold a lot of them to pay for rented pastures. We sold more. Temperatures rose into the nineties by April year after year. The hot winds blew. The ground steamed and dried up within hours after the rare storms. Whole forests died or burned.

So when Spring, real, honest Spring, with rain,

ABOVE: This is what Spring still looks like in a large exclosure ungrazed since the 1940s. Almost all plants in this photo are toxic, semitoxic or too sharp and spiky to be good wildlife habitat. Located across the fence from the author's ranch, this site is in what scientists now call a "steady state" which no amount of rest will improve. Please note the abundant cryptogamic crust which is alleged by anti-ranching activists to be a great seedbed for native grasses.
LEFT: Native flowers are just one of the many rewards of well-managed grazing. Photos © Steven H. Rich

came at last, John was pretty doggoned happy driving our thirty-seven remaining cattle out into the beauty and abundance. He wanted to share the moment.

Spring still does not come to our "rested" land. After the wettest Winter and Spring in a long time, the main effect in the "protected" rested areas has been to grow a small amount of toxic tansy mustard, some burr buttercups—sharp, spiky little devils about an inch long—with a few other annuals totaling perhaps fifteen to fifty pounds per acre. This is compared to 250 to 2,000 pounds of rich grass and flowers on the managed ranch country. I'm sure that in the Fall some of the sage will grow seeds for the harvester ants. The rested areas are in what scientists now call a steady, stable or persis-

tent state. It can stay that way, barren and eroding, until all the soil is gone.

I read years ago that grass is a sign of God's mercy. It sure feels that way to me. So does globe mallow, the beautiful orange-blossomed plant that deer, rabbits and pronghorns love so much. So do four-wing saltbush, asters, buckwheat and so many others that spread into the land we bulldozed, plowed, burned, seeded, then grazed.

Most of us who graze livestock do so with great care and a deep sense of responsibility. Along with a lot of others, I've worked to share this knowledge for almost thirty years. I know from deep experience that when ranchers, environmentalists, government agency people and any other concerned citizens work together to bless nature by letting the ecosystem itself guide them instead of projecting their own dogma onto the land, they always bring healing and biodiversity. As they observe and learn, they get better at it.

The pattern of healing on the ground spreads into the community, resulting in prosperity and wonderful days spent together. Mercy for the land caused Dad to wheedle us into this adventure, along with a desire to see us grow and learn about nature with our own butts on the line. Love of nature is a bond John and our family share with all other humans (in the original "humane" sense of the word).

It would not surprise Mad Baggins at all to find that the first and chief skill in directly healing lands is to view each other mercifully and kindly. Cognitive clarity follows that and, before long, springtime, grass, flowers and abundance return to land from which they have long been absent.

Steven H. Rich is president of Rangeland Restoration Academy in Salt Lake City, Utah. He can be reached at <steve@rangelandrestoration.org>.

"Here are ten cows feeding on the hill beside me.
Why do they move about so fast as they feed? They have
advanced thirty rods in ten minutes, and sometimes the one
runs to keep up. Is it to give the grass thus a chance to grow
more equally and always get a fresh bite?"

HENRY DAVID THOREAU, JOURNAL, MAY 15, 1853

*Cows serenely graze the southern Sierra Nevada hills
near Springville, California, as they have for centuries.
Where they roam, wildlife abounds and carpets of
flowers cloak the hills in Spring. Photo © Carolyn Fox*

Art Rogers, pride and joy

North Carolina-born Art Rogers uses his camera to document ranches and rural communities, and the people who live in them, especially in the area of California just north of San Francisco. "The remaining farmlands in Marin are truly unique," he says. "They are part of the culture and legacy of the Bay Area. They are worth saving."

Rogers lives with his wife and two daughters in Point Reyes Station California. His work has won fellowships from the Guggenheim, the National Endowment for the Arts and the Marin Arts Council, and is in major collections. <www.artrogers.com>

Clarence and Nancy Wright, sheep ranchers, Healdsburg, California. Clarence was born on this ranch in 1913. He and Nancy ran about 350 sheep until the 1980s when they couldn't control the coyotes, so they switched to cows. When Clarence passed away in 1986, his son took over the family business. Photo © Art Rogers / Pt. Reyes

Gary Pile and three little pigs, Mook, Kentucky. Gary's parents raised pigs, among other things, on their Kentucky farm. When Gary went to England to study how the English raised pigs by isolating them from others so they don't catch as many diseases, he came back home and converted to that method—to the chagrin of the old-timers who preferred the old way. But, to Gary, "the new breed," was more productive. Photo © Art Rogers / Pt. Reyes

"*How well-behaved are cows!
When they approach me
reclining in the shade, from
curiosity, or to receive a whisp
of grass, or to share the shade,
or to lick the dog held up, like a
calf, though just now they ran
at him to toss him, they do not
obtrude. Their company is
acceptable, for they can endure
the longest pause; they have
not got to be entertained.*"

HENRY DAVID THOREAU,
JOURNAL, 1852

*The road to Point Reyes, California.
When the Point Reyes Peninsula
became The Point Reyes National
Seashore in the 1960s, all the dairy
and beef ranchers agreed to sell
the government their land but
negotiated lifetime-plus leases so
they could continue ranching.
Photo © Art Rogers / Pt. Reyes*

*George Nunes and his triplet calves, Point Reyes,
California. There is one chance in one million of
triplet calves being born and surviving.
Photo © Art Rogers / Pt. Reyes*

Louie Ricci, livestock auctioneer, Santa Rosa, California.
Louie has been auctioning a variety of livestock for fifty-nine
years and is still going strong. Photo © Art Rogers / Pt. Reyes

Virgil Trujillo hands a rope to his fourteen-year-old son, Ventura. Trujillo roots reach back to 1754 in the Abiquiu area of New Mexico. Photo © Gene Peach

Learning the ropes

WORDS AND PHOTOS © GENE PEACH.

Ranch kids are the living proof of the continuity of the cowboy way of life. Their spirit belongs to the land and they possess a firsthand knowledge of animals their urban counterparts will never know. They are modern children connecting to a natural world through early meaningful work, traditional values and partnerships with animals. This generation of ranch children should be celebrated. They are the future of the West.

Coley Barner's getting ready to saddle his horse, Dusty, on the Lucy Ranch. Coley's dad manages both the Lucy Ranch and the 777 Ranch with a total of over 89,000 acres. Thirteen-year-old Coley also "neighbors" on other ranches in New Mexico's Torrance County. Photo © Gene Peach

Six-year-old Austin Vincent lives on the ranch where his grandmother was born. There are New Mexico cowboys in every branch of the family which has been in Union County for five generations. Photo © Gene Peach

111

Jordan Muncy has been in the saddle for five years—since she was three. Her grandmother rode bulls in the rodeo. Her parents met while competing in rodeos. Photo © Gene Peach

Wild Bunch Rodeo Company supplies bulls and broncs for rodeos and the Danley family travels together, sometimes hundreds of miles. Seven-year-old Dakota cleans a hoof, just a regular part of horse care. Photo © Gene Peach

Coley Barner and Matthew Connell on the Lucy Ranch. They're taking a break after helping to pen nearly a thousand yearlings. **Photo © Gene Peach**

Six-year-old Bryce Howe has been riding on the remote Howe Ranch near the Texas border since he was able to sit a saddle. With his ten-year-old brother, Hadley, he travels thirty miles to school. **Photo © Gene Peach**

These photos appear in "Making a Hand: Growing Up Cowboy in New Mexico," photography by Gene Peach, text by Max Evans, introduction by Elmer Kelton. Copyright 2005. Published by Museum of New Mexico Press, 800-249-7737, <www.mnmpress.org>.

Early turnout to a dry spring

© CAROLYN DUFURRENA

All the promise of the new season withers
In sullen gray clouds that refuse
To share their moisture.
We raise our eyes to the north,
Scan skies for a promise
Of rain,
Breathe in the hope
Of that wet desert smell.
No.
Not today.

Springs in the high country draw on old
water deep inside.
I cross the ridge in January,
A skiff of dry snow dusting
The road I've only known
In summer.

We open the gates. The calves gambol out
Kicking up dust
Where the fuzz of green grass
Should be.
I watch cattle turn back and look at me,
As if asking, "Now? Already?
Are you sure?"

Herefords at the
Pitchfork Ranch in a
West Texas winter.
Yeah, it snows in Texas!
Photo © Bob Moorhouse

James Gholson gets ready to ride out in late Fall to check cattle at the Pitchfork Ranch in West Texas. It will be a quiet ride in a gentle snowstorm. Photo © Bob Moorhouse

Henry Real Bird

PHOTOS © PETER DE LORY. WORDS © HAL CANNON.

Henry "Hank" Real Bird is a Crow Indian. He's also a cowboy who lives on the family ranch in the Wolf Teeth Mountains of Montana. He raises bucking horse mares with his brothers. And to boot, he's a poet and a teacher. That's the simple part of explaining who Henry Real Bird is. He is also the most compassionate person I've ever met. He says he's been to the bottom and floated back. What this means is that he understands the pain and struggle of those around him. He does his part for his tribe. He lives a spiritual life. His poems are prayers. They are for people incapacitated by alcohol and drugs. They are for struggling schoolkids on reservations. And they are the script for a reenactment of the Battle of Little Big Horn that he and his brothers produce at the end of June each year right on the river where the battle took place. Henry Real Bird perches high, as the Crow flies.

Henry Real Bird's ranch is a forty-mile drive into the Wolf Teeth Mountains above Crow Agency, Montana. He often rides through country where the Battle of the Little Big Horn was fought.
Photo © Peter de Lory

Henry Real Bird, holding a ceremonial pipe, came up to this place with an axe and shovel and built his home. He says there's nothing like the feeling of seeing smoke from your own stovepipe.
Photo © Peter de Lory

Cowboys and friends are moving John Ascuaga's herd of 1,200 mother cows sixty miles from Summer range in Bridgeport, California, to Winter feed at the home ranch in Smith, Nevada. The drive will take four days. Riding point until they get the herd out in the brush, from left: Terry Sullivan, Chance Gee, Jamie Sommer Gee, cousin Dave Sommer, Don Spanier and Kent Davis. John Ascuaga is riding the drag with brother Frank and son Steve. Photo © C.J. Hadley

Nebraska, lives of tradition

WORDS AND PHOTOS © CHARLES W. GUILDNER.

The core of my "Lives of Tradition" photographic project is finding and recording ordinary people who are living and working in some ways that have changed little since the settling of the heartland of this country. This has brought me to the study of farmers and ranchers and small rural communities where the people are living

Branding on the Haythorn Ranch near Arthur, Nebraska. A threatening sky with sun breaks and a brisk breeze, cloud shadows scudding across the landscape and cowboys bringing in the herd for the morning branding seemed to contain all the elements for a special photograph. Waiting and watching for the shadows and the shafts of light to all play together, especially illuminating the branding, resulted in this image. What a day! Photo © Charles W. Guildner

Rick Gaudrault has been cowboying in the Midwest for over twenty-five years at the Sunlight Ranch near Wyola, Montana; the Padlock Ranch, Ranchester, Wyoming; the Haythorn Ranch, Arthur, Nebraska; and the Bartlett Ranch, LaGrange, Wyoming. Rick is an all-around cowboy but has a particular interest in training horses for ranch work. Photo © Charles W. Guildner

Floyd Bacon has been cowboying most of his life and is all cowboy. I knew from the first time I met him that I wanted to make his portrait. After knowing and watching him for several days during branding, I asked to make this photograph. Floyd has a cup of coffee in his hand any time he is not in the saddle. He asked me if I wanted him to put the cup down. Oh no, I said. It would not be you without that cup. Photo © Charles W. Guildner

Buck Buckles feeds in a blizzard, Gordon, Nebraska, 2004. At five a.m. on Easter morning, while harnessing the horses, there was no snow on the ground. Forty-five minutes later it was snowing hard. Photo © Charles W. Guildner

these "lives of tradition." Many of these lifestyles are shrinking in numbers, so it is interesting to find people whose lives seem grounded in tradition, who find their vitality in long-standing ways of living. How long many of these traditional ways will continue is uncertain. But the spirit I have found among these people suggests many will continue.

I travel and live in my pickup truck camper, visiting previous

Mary Bell Cooksley, Berwyn, Nebraska. Mary Bell, born September 12, 1920, married Leo Cooksley in 1942. In 1876, her granduncle Theo Frischkorn homesteaded some of the land Mary Bell now ranches and built the house in which she lives. The barn in this photograph was built in the 1940s from the oak flooring of Bernard's Dance Pavilion south of Broken Bow. Photo © Charles W. Guildner

Mary Ann and Katherine Kelly, 2003. Katherine, age seventeen, and Mary Ann, age fifteen, are the daughters of Thomas and Arlene Kelly. The Kelly family operates the Cocklebur Ranch near the old pioneer town of Rock Falls, located near Atlanta, Nebraska. Excellent riders and cowhands, the girls ride bareback much of the time and are also trick ropers. They are homeschooled and do much of the ranch work, rarely missing a day on horseback. Photo © Charles W. Guildner

Justin Bradley, Brewster, Nebraska, has been a cowboy all his life and is steeped in the tradition of cowboying and ranching. He grew up in Cheyenne, Oklahoma, and moved to Brewster, Nebraska, where he lives with his wife Tracy and sons Blayne and JT. He works on the Rhoades Ranch near Brewster. Photo © Charles W. Guildner

Moving camp. Being a sailor, this beautiful June day in the rolling Sandhill rangeland of Nebraska, with a good breeze and the sun reflecting off the grasses and ridges, reminded me of the spindrift off the tops of the waves at sea. Branding roundup at the Haythorn Ranch near Arthur, Nebraska, requires nearly three weeks to complete. Long established traditional methods including chuck wagon camp and woodfire branding are used. Camp is maintained for two or three days before moving to the next branding location. Photo © Charles W. Guildner

and new locations, following leads, and networking to find new people and places where traditions are sustained. I photograph almost daily for three to four months, beginning in April, returning home in July. The rest of the year is spent working with new negatives, making prints, corresponding with new leads, and making preparations for going "On the Road Again."

Con Flynn and Jim Owens sit and talk at the Shasta Livestock Auction in Cottonwood, northern California. Ranching stays in the blood and the auction house serves as a social gathering place for ranchers both working and retired. Photo © Joel Sartore

"*Don't matter the size of the hat or the age of the cowboy, there's always a moment to set and chat and maybe spin a tall tale or two. It's a way to pass on what you know and what you hanker for. It's a way to keep the past connected to the future.*"

BARBARA WIES, 2005

Oregon Roaring Springs Ranch children rest on the tongue of a chuck wagon in Frenchglen, Oregon. Photo © Larry Turner

Bridging the rural-urban divide

© RICHARD L. KNIGHT, Ph.D.

The fundamental chasm separating rural and urban communities is that urban Americans don't seem to care where their food comes from while taking for granted the open space and healthy watersheds that ranchers care for. Our increasingly global economy makes it difficult for ranchers to compete with cheap food grown offshore, and our urban public hasn't figured out how to compensate ranchers for the healthy land and wildlife habitat they provide.

We have severed the historic covenant that bound rural and urban people together. In the past we knew where food came from and supported it. We valued the services that rural people provided. Urban people need food, and highly value open space. Ranchers produce both. To the degree that this natural interdependency can be reconstituted, the economics of ranching should flourish.

As my friend rangeland ecologist Pete Sundt is fond of saying: "There is a widespread belief in America today that lands should not be used for economic purposes, but should be conserved or restored to 'the way they were'."

Because of our enviable position on top of the world's global economy we can have our cake and eat it too. But what hypocrites this makes us. By importing our food, fiber, minerals, energy and wood products, we simply export the ecological costs to developing nations that have neither the laws to protect their resources nor the will to do so.

It also opens us up to threats to our nation's security. Note that 2004 was the first year that America imported more food than it exported. A secure homeland is not the country with the greatest military. Home, land, security is where urban people realize that ecologically sustainable ranching is possible. They realize that rural cultures matter—and urban people are prepared to compensate ranchers for protecting open space, wildlife habitat and watersheds through land stewardship, and for producing healthy food.

Building bridges across this rural-urban divide will reconnect us with each other and ensure that America's homeland will always be secure. A first step is to connect food production to open space, wildlife habitat and watershed protection, both economically and ecologically. This will allow Americans to eat locally produced food on land that is well stewarded. Ranchers should be compensated for healthy food grown on healthy lands.

Writer and Kentucky farmer Wendell Berry had it right when he said: "The most tragic conflict in the history of conservation is that between environmentalists and the farmers and ranchers. It is tragic because it is unnecessary. There is no irresolvable conflict here, but the conflict that exists can be resolved only on the basis of a common understanding of good practice. Here again we need to study and foster working models: farms and ranches that are knowledgeably striving to bring economic practice into line with ecological reality, and local food economies in which consumers conscientiously support the best land stewardship."

Ranchers are symbolic of what can be, not just for rural communities, but for all America. For security's sake, it's time to beat the swords into plowshares.

Richard L. Knight is a professor of wildlife conservation at Colorado State University. His eighth book is "Ranching West of the 100th Meridian." Rick and his wife Heather live and neighbor in the Livermore Valley of Colorado.

As long as the people in the tract houses think hamburgers and shakes come from Mickey D's, this bovine is in trouble. America's food and fiber producers are also the caretakers of healthy grassland, woodlands, lakes and streams. Americans should look for locally produced food on land that is well-stewarded, to the benefit of all. Photo © Twainhart Hill

"*I can remember one Spring when a late blizzard hit our lambing corrals in the desert. There were only a few roofed sheds, not nearly enough to cover a few thousand ewes having their lambs at all hours of the day or night. The lambs were born in open corrals whipped and soaked by sleeting snow. We could do nothing else but drag them with sheep hooks to the flimsy protection of a corral fence, and hope they lived until the storm passed and the sun came out.*"

ROBERT LAXALT, "SWEET PROMISED LAND," UNIVERSITY OF NEVADA PRESS, 1957

"Dusky white shapes mutter to each other; brass bells sound in the sagebrush. They move slowly, easing away from the human shapes standing silently, guiding them toward the corral. The sun pours light through the dust as they funnel toward the gate, mill around softly, calling their lambs." Carolyn Dufurrena, "Fifty Miles from Home," University of Nevada Press, 2002.
Photo © Linda Dufurrena

The lamb is innocently curious; the cat is not amused.
Photo © Linda Dufurrena

"Her Chance to Dance" is a tribute to the American cowgirl. It shows that when given the chance she will show her stuff. The model for it is my daughter, Calla. She has won numerous awards for cutting, including Colorado State High School Champion three years in a row.

Tim Cox

Tim Cox has achieved the goal he set for himself at age five "to be a cowboy artist." His most recent awards include the Express Ranches Great American Cowboy Award and the coveted Prix de West Purchase Award from the National Academy of Western Art. A cattle rancher and horse trainer, Cox paints the world he knows and loves. However vast and beautiful his landscapes, his delight in the subject shines through. Tim's comments about the paintings on these pages clearly show how deeply his heart is in his work. <www.timcox.com>

"If Looks Could Kill." I was breaking this horse for an artist friend. He educated me about everything bad a horse can do. I had tried everything I know about—the "make the right thing easy, the wrong thing hard" method of working with a bronc. He made everything difficult. He woke up in a different world about every few minutes. There was no love lost between the two of us.

"In the Bronc Corral." This is my bronc corral at Eagle Creek, Arizona. I made it out of cedar posts. It is round and stout. I use it to catch colts and start riding them their first few saddles.

"*While there are many things you can fake through in this life, pretending that you know horses when you don't isn't one of them.*"

COOKIE McCLUNG,
"HORSE FOLK ARE DIFFERENT"

Wrangle horses, four a.m. Tough, black coffee. Breakfast, four-thirty. It is still predawn when Spanish Ranch buckaroos head out of their roundup camp to gather cattle in the Fall on the high desert ranges of northern Nevada. Photo © C.J. Hadley

"Rose about five. Had early breakfast. Got my housework done about nine. Baked six loaves of bread. Made a kettle of mush and have now a suet pudding and beef boiling. My girl [Indian] has ironed and I have managed to put my clothes away and set my house in order. May the merciful be with me through the unexpected scene. Nine o'clock p.m. was delivered of another son."

DIARY OF MARY RICHARDSON WALKER, 1830s, FROM "WESTWARD THE WOMEN"
BY NANCY WILSON ROSS, NORTH POINT PRESS, 1985

Woman with rifle in doorway of her claim shack, Newell, South Dakota, ca. 1911. Photo © Tom Robinson

She's been described as a "five-foot four-inch mass of muscle and sinew, like rawhide that is dried or cured…gentle with animals and feminine in the best sense of the word." Melody Harding of the Bar Cross Ranch, Big Piney, Wyoming, grew up on a ranch as an only child and is deeply knowledgeable about every aspect of ranching. "So you age a little faster [working on a ranch] than you would normally," she says. "That's the least you can pay for a good life. At least you're in a wholesome atmosphere and you're doing something worthwhile." Photo © Barbara Van Cleve

For a kid, the ranch is a cornucopia of times to treasure. Hardworking dogs are also loving and gentle companions. Horses need care, but they give it back in full measure. Even roping provides opportunity to learn a skill you can show off at the ranch rodeo.
Photo © Larry Angier

Three-year-old David Steeves gets a horse nuzzling while his eleven-year-old sister Lindy rides in the background, Crane, Oregon.
Photo © Larry Turner

"Ranching is the best possible way to live—a great way for kids to grow up learning responsibility. Kids know they are necessary; they are respected; they gain a strong sense of self-worth and family unity."

MICHELLE CARROCCIA IN "HARD TWIST. WESTERN RANCH WOMEN" BY BARBARA VAN CLEVE,
MUSEUM OF NEW MEXICO PRESS, 1995

*Daylan Harness, Big Loop Roping Event,
Jordan Valley, Oregon. Photo © Larry Turner*

Deep roots

WORDS © BARBARA WIES.
PHOTO: ROSS HUMPHREYS © JIM CHILTON.

Chilton roots run deep in Arizona's ranching community. Ken Chilton (shown with sons Jim on left and Tom on right) is a fourth-generation Arizona rancher. Since 1905, when the U.S. Forest Service replaced "open range" with regulated private allotments, the Chiltons have been careful to stock conservatively while improving the land, providing more forage for wildlife, and encouraging native trees and grasses to flourish.

"A cowboy's creed is honesty, integrity and straightforwardness," Jim Chilton says. "Ranching is a unique western American way of life and a national cultural treasure worthy of preservation."

Renowned range management expert and environmental advocate Dr. Jerry Holechek of New Mexico State University found the Chilton allotment to have "the richest, most diverse flora of any area I have ever worked in." Hydrologist Dr. William Fleming declared the allotment's riparian areas "a success story."

Wildlife sharing the Chilton grazing lands include javelina, deer, coatimundi, songbirds and Mearns quail. Jim's wife Sue, an ardent amateur naturalist and member of the Arizona Game and Fish Commission, says "there is absolutely no inherent incompatibility between raising livestock and providing habitat for wildlife. A good ranch is good for both."

Buckaroo

BY BOB BOYD

Photos from the exhibition catalog for "Buckaroo! The Hispanic Heritage of the High Desert"

Cowboy, cowpuncher or buckaroo, each has a unique style and culture. For over a century, the rangeland of the Great Basin (eastern California, Nevada, southwestern Idaho and eastern Oregon) has been home to the buckaroo.

Following the Spanish conquest of Mexico, many conquistadors established great estates on the vast plains surrounding Mexico City. They employed trusted Indians and mixed-blood mestizos. As riders on the cattle ranges of Mexico, they roped using hand-braided rawhide reatas, a craft brought by the Moors from Spain.

Called vaqueros, "those who work the cattle," these horsemen accompanied expeditions to the farthest reaches of Spanish colonial exploration and conquest, to Texas, New Mexico and California.

The evolution of vaquero gear continued, from finely tooled saddles to rawhide gear, silver inlaid spurs and Santa Barbara spade bits.

At the conclusion of the Mexican-American War in 1848, American rule came to California. Young vaqueros whose fathers had worked for the missions or ranchos now rode for "gringo" bosses. Riding alongside the Hispanic and Indian vaqueros were young Anglo-American and European immigrants. The newcomers looked to

Frank Morgan stood for this studio portrait in 1930, proudly showing off his silver inlaid Santa Barbara-style spade bit and hand-braided rawhide reins. He was twenty-five. The Oregon native spent a lifetime buckarooing at ranches across the High Desert. He died at eighty, bucked off a horse while roping at a branding. Studio photo by R.W. Heck. Photo © Tom Robinson

the old Californios as models of horsemanship and civility.

With trucks and trailers and the economics of ranching, there are fewer buckaroos on the remaining big outfits. Many believe that the old ways will endure. Men and women, boys and girls on western ranches today, are all on horseback when the need arises. Many, regardless of gender or age, are as graceful with a reata, light-handed with a bridle horse, and as competent as a vaquero of a century ago.

Onetime buckaroo boss of the P Ranch, vaquero Raphael "Chappo" Remudas, poses near Burns, Oregon, about 1890. The word "vaquero" gradually became "buckaroo." Photo © Harney County Historical Museum, Burns, Oregon

At the Whitehorse Ranch in southeastern Oregon, Ken Bentz is "heeling" a calf for branding. The ranch was established in 1869. Photo © Kurt Markus

An early land-grant family, the Lugos, wear traditional Californio clothing in 1888. Their Hispanic heritage, horsemanship and ranching skills inspired the buckaroo culture on the High Desert. Photo © Seaver Center for Western History Research, Natural History Museum of Los Angeles County, Los Angeles, California

Bob Wroten's bridle horse at the McDermitt Fourth of July Stampede in Nevada. This responsive horse was trained in the vaquero style with hackamore and spade bit. Photo © Kurt Markus

Bob Boyd is western history curator at High Desert Museum in Bend, Oregon. The text and photos are from "Buckaroo: The Hispanic Heritage of the High Desert," an exhibition that attracted a quarter million visitors in its first year. In January 2005, "Buckaroo" opened at the Western Folklife Center in Elko, Nevada, where it will be on view through December 2009.

146

The vaquero wore a flat-brimmed, low-crowned Stetson fashioned after those popular in the early 1800s. The spurs are Californio-style, too, from about 1870. The vaquero's hand-braided rawhide reata could be one hundred feet long. Photos © Thomas Osborne

Hackamore horse at the ZX Ranch, Paisley, Oregon. The horse wears a braided rawhide bosal and twisted horsehair mecate. The buckaroo wears packer boots and silver inlaid spurs with large rowells. His chinks and saddle are adorned with silver conchos. Photo © Kurt Markus

Journey in the land of purple shadows

BY IDAH MEACHAM STROBRIDGE. EDITED BY CAROLYN DUFURRENA.

Nine-year-old Laura Idah Meacham came with her family to Nevada's Lassen Valley in 1864. From their cattle ranch, they watched covered wagons lumbering west to California or south toward the mines of Nevada. With the completion of the cross-continent railroad in 1868, Idah's father opened his Humboldt House Hotel. Trains stopped there to allow passengers to dine. In 1877, Idah went to California to finish her education. She returned to Nevada in 1884 with her new husband, Sam Strobridge. The cattle market collapsed in 1885. Harsh winters followed, killing ninety-five percent of Nevada's cattle. By 1889, Idah's husband and three sons were dead. Idah made the choice to stay on with her parents at the Humboldt House "to live a life utterly without pretense." She and her father established a bookbinding business, and Idah launched a new career as a writer. She died in 1932.—Carolyn Dufurrena

If you love the mountains, you count the cliffs and chasms among old friends one loves long and well. The clefts and canyons of the Coast Ranges and the Sierra are dark and beautiful with pine and tamarack and fir. But what of those far back from the sea, that lie in purple mountains far to the east, where gray foothills slide down to meet the stark white of the playa? Do you know these canyons?

It is not where human life and human interests are found, but in the little-known, the passed-by and forgotten places that one feels the power of these mountains.

The ranges are furrowed and gashed by ravines and gorges where the sun comes late and leaves in early afternoon. Their sides are hollowed into hiding places of repose and calm. Here, one goes hand in hand with Nature.

"The ranges are furrowed and gashed by ravines and gorges where the sun comes late and leaves in early afternoon," Idah Meacham Strobridge wrote. "Their sides are hollowed into hiding places of repose and calm. Here, one goes hand in hand with Nature." Photo © Linda Dufurrena

In Springtime they are fair, as all things are fair when fresh with youth; but it is in Autumn when one finds every shade of fire and blood that they are at their best. Some canyons are bare of color, and you may turn your horse's head up one of these on some Autumn day, and find only scattered clumps of buck-brush and willow. Beneath these are hidden springs which keep the sparse shade green through the hot summer, the roots moist and growing.

Grass grows here—a patch of wild rye browned by the suns of summer. Rabbitbrush, nettles, hore-hound are brown and dead. White butterflies flutter above weeds that bloom with blossoms of gold.

The thistles and mariposa lilies which grew white and purple up and down the canyon have dry seed pods now.

How still this world is. The only sounds are your horse's hooves, his labored breathing as he climbs, the creak of saddle leather.

As he begins the steeper ascent your fingers twist into his mane. Higher and higher you climb, up and still up, to reach the dividing ridge, where you can give your horse a breathing spell. As he stands, your eyes rise to the summit's rugged peaks that, with all your climbing, seem as far away as ever.

The cliffs are carved and hewn into arch and architrave by the elements in the hands of Time.

An avalanche of rock has fallen and left an arch so wide, so high, that a great patch of the deep blue sky shines through. Three chariots abreast could pass beneath its span.

How you long to climb, to be there alone in the awful stillness of those heights where God speaks to one through the silence. But the sun is slanting into the West. You descend, into a gorge so deep that the sun finds its granite-gravelled floor only at midday. Water overflows the stony rim of a mill-dam, tumbling down in a glittering, sparkling spray over the neglected flume that in years past gave power to the mill a mile or two down the canyon. Silent now, at rest.

The creek is bordered with rose thickets, and wild plum, walled with tall cliffs that throw long purple-black shadows on the sheer walls of cliffs that face them.

Down the canyon you ride. In the wet places, late columbines are growing, mallows not yet gone to seed. Half an acre of wild poppies toss their thin white petals to the breeze.

Fine feathery grasses grow at the base of a great granite boulder. The skeleton branches of a dead bush show as delicate as a bit of sea-moss against it. Gnarled, rough-twisted, stripped of bark, a dead juniper leans fallen on the boulder. How long since it came tumbling down this ravine?

The moments pass—you forget to reckon Time. A pebble rolls down the hillside. You sit up and look intently, but there is nothing moving, only the gray granite of rocks and bushes of stunted sage.

For a full minute or more, you watch in intent silence. Then to yourself you say: "No, there's nothing there." You lie back. Instinctively you feel something watching you—something that notes your every movement. Nothing breaks the uniform gray of the smooth slope, the supreme silence.

There! Something is moving after all, something that a moment ago your eyes rested on, among the sagebrush of the hillside. Now you see the sage hen, coming carefully to the spring. A dozen times in the past ten minutes you looked right at her, so like the bushes of these hills that she seems to be one of them. How slowly she picks her way. She has seen you, but she keeps coming bravely to the spring for her afternoon drink.

As you raise yourself on your arm, there is a whir of wings. She sails away over the ridge, and whir, whir, there go two others and then a dozen more. Soon the entire flock, a score or more, sweeps over the ridge into the next ravine.

Away down, perhaps half a dozen miles below you on the valley floor, a freight train creeps along twin threads of shining steel. You are so close here to

the civilized world, and yet so remote from the petty meannesses of life.

Stand a moment in the shadow of a porphyry cliff, lean your face against the cool whiteness of a quartz seam. Imagine what is hidden hundreds of feet down beneath this spot. Wonder where it will be in a

thousand years. Will the solitude of the canyons still be unbroken, or changed with all else in a world made of changes?

You raise your eyes aloft and look into the measureless deep of the darkening heavens. Faint stars are coming in the twilight sky.

The Calico Mountains at the west end of Nevada's Black Rock Desert. In the stony mountains of the high desert nestle secret springs and hidden meadows that bloom with wildflowers and ripple with grasses. "The moments pass," Idah wrote, "you forget to reckon Time." Photo © Linda Dufurrena

The O6

WORDS AND PHOTOS © DIANE LACY

The rugged, beautiful Kokernot O6 Ranch established by my husband's great-grandfather H.L. Kokernot in 1883 has been run by the Kokernot-Lacy family ever since. This cattle ranch in the Davis Mountains of far west Texas is our heritage, our life and our passion.

At an elevation of 6,000 feet, the 220-square-mile ranch has moun-

Moving cattle "off the top" from Black Canyon to headquarters during Fall roundup. The cowboy is making sure that the drag follows the leaders.

In the sorting pen at Willow Springs. This pen is used a couple of times a year before shipping. This neat spot has a view of Polk's Peak.

In the Fall, O6 cowboys camp out for a month during roundup, with about sixteen in the saddle to gather 3,000 head of cattle. There are two camp cooks. After a hard day, the cowboys relax before chuck, watching a long-awaited and welcome storm coming.

tains, canyons and vast grasslands between Fort Davis and Alpine, Texas. A traditional, commercial cow-calf operation, we run one cow to forty acres during rainy years. After fifteen years of drought, longest in recorded history, we now run about one cow to one hundred acres.

We actually raise grass. Our cattle, horses and wildlife are the tools for harvesting and marketing grass in a southwest desert environment not

suitable for farming or anything else. Cattle ranching is a good way to utilize the rich, native gramma grass of our mountain pastures.

Since the popularity of "reality" shows, we've been asked to tell the real story of ranching without all the romance. The romance is what keeps you hanging on to this crazy way of life. If you take the romance out of ranching, no one would do it, at least not for the long haul in a business filled with impossible odds: severe drought, unpredictable prices, over-

Rod DeVoll runs the roundup crew, knows the country, and understands cattle. He has worked for the O6 for twenty years.

A cowboy holds the remuda while the cow boss catches his mount for the day's work. He'll choose one with a long trot for the morning gather.

There's a special relationship between horses and men. Here Tommy Vaughn pets his buddy after turning him loose for the day.

regulation, an out-of-control Endangered Species Act, hard physical labor, low wages and high overhead costs.

The closest I can come to reality on the O6 is through my candid photography. I try to describe what it is like to ride out with sixteen cowboys before daylight, spread out around a twenty-section pasture and wait for first light to start the gather, eat off the chuck wagon and sleep in a

At the end of a roundup day, the horses are turned loose to drink, graze and rest. This cowboy is about to unsaddle his mount and brush him out at Number Five Camp in the northern mountains close to Major Peak.

Cowboy bookkeeping. Donnie Slover uses a typical way to keep records by writing on his hand—counting cattle through the gate, how many calves branded and cut, how many mothers with new babies dropped back from the drive, and how many horses needed for the day's work.

teepee for a month during Fall and Spring roundups.

But a photograph lacks the smell of everything fresh, sweet and clean after a rain; the taste of Marcus's steaks, camp bread and cobbler cooked in Dutch ovens on hot coals around the chuck wagon; the sound of a herd of horses running, hooves striking rocks in the silence of the dawn, or deep rolling thunder echoing through a canyon; and the thrill of seeing a calf or colt being born,

or being humbled by riding alone under an enormous sky and miles of spectacular scenery with nothing man-made to interrupt the natural beauty.

O6 ranch life is also about relationships. We have loyal hands who

After a long, hot day's work during Spring branding, these members of the O6 remuda are turned loose. They head straight for the trough.

The good life. High mountain pastures are home for the horses. This grassy country is at 6,000 feet in the North Webster mountain pasture, about fifty miles of good O6 Ranch country between Fort Davis and Alpine, Texas.

The cowboys below have been horseback since way before daylight, gathering cattle. On a cold day a few will hold the herd while the others take a quick coffee break around the campfire. Pretty soon they'll catch new mounts to use for cutting the herd for shipping. They will separate the cattle into two main groups: mothers with heifer calves and mothers with steer calves.

have worked for us for a long time. They are part of our family and take pride in riding for the brand. My husband's mother and his sisters, their children and our children and grandchildren all have a part of the ownership and operation of the ranch. We feel proud to be producers of food, fiber and byproducts that are essential for quality of life. Somehow this all outweighs the hardship and we thank God every day that we can be part of the legacy of the O6.

Chris Lacy, part owner and manager of the O6, has just caught "Smoky Buddha," his best cutting horse. This good gelding knows he's the best horse in the O6 remuda and he's ready to cut and sort the herd for shipping.

Chris' wife, Diane Lacy, is an award-winning western photographer whose work is in museums and private and corporate collections around the world. For more information about the ranch and photographs online: <www.06ranch.com>.

*Jeff, Laurel, Royce and Lisa Hanson,
Maggie Creek Ranch, Nevada, 1982.
I met this wonderful family at Maggie
Creek, where I rode and worked cattle
with Royce and the buckaroo crew.
Royce and Laurel now run the ranch in
southern Montana that the legendary
writer and artist Will James once
owned. Lisa and her husband have a
business in California. Jeff built
fine saddles for years while
he buckarooed in the Great Basin
area. Now he's a full-time
saddlemaker in Monticello, Utah.
Photo © Jay Dusard*

Beautiful Gibbonsville Road runs through the Eleven Twenty Ranch and passes over the Continental Divide. When traveling from Wisdom, Montana, the winding gravel road is still used as a shortcut to Gibbonsville, Idaho. It's convenient, as long as you realize hair-raising turns and double-black-diamond vertical drops are in your travel plans. Don't even think of pulling a horse trailer. Photo © Cynthia Baldauf

Antelope at twilight. Antelope, mule deer, mountain lion, bobcat, coyote, sage grouse, chukar, quail, fox, rattlesnake and raptors share range with the livestock, Dufurrena Sheep and Cattle Company, Denio, Nevada. Photo © Linda Dufurrena

"I can't say I was disappointed when people started catching on about how Disney morphed nature into an easily understood amusement park. I felt the same compassion for Thumper and Bambi and all their pals, and laughed like everybody else at the antics of otters, but I knew it wasn't all that simple and that if I might catch a fat bunny in my sights while hunting one day, I wouldn't hesitate. Sorry, Thumper. Really. It's a choice I had as the top of the food chain, and even if I would never abuse it by killing more than I needed to survive, I cannot lie about the power I felt over life all around me. Like all predators, I was most dangerous when I was hungry. Giving food a name wouldn't make me starve."

TIM FINDLEY, 2005

Movin' on out

PHOTOS © C.J. HADLEY

The YP Ranch runs cattle in northeastern Nevada, using good open range heading out onto the Owyhee Desert in southern Idaho. In Spring, during greenup, the buckaroos take many days and dozens of cavvy horses to drop the cows off, a few hundred at a time, to feed on the nutritious, high desert grasses. One or two buckaroos will watch the cattle during Summer and doctor them when necessary. They make sure the livestock—and wildlife—have water, and, at the right time, move them to new ground. The whole crew will gather the cows and calves to bring them back home for shipping in the Fall.

During the Spring turnout and Fall gather, the buckaroos stay at Stateline Camp. When the day's work is done the cowboys might break colts, practice roping, braid rawhide reins or reatas by kerosene lamp, or twist horsehair into pretty ropes called mecates. Some of the best times are when stories are shared around the campfire.

YP buckaroos start moving the herd toward Stateline Camp and disbursement over some big and beautiful open country. Photo © C.J. Hadley

Cow boss Doug Groves is one of the West's best rawhide braiders. He is also an expert in cattle, horses, and dogs. Photo © C.J. Hadley

"It takes forty years to learn how to work cattle, but you can go to Philadelphia and learn to be a lawyer in eight."

WAYLAND NEWBERRY, FOREMAN, TURKEY TRACK RANCH, NEW MEXICO, 1999,
BEST REMUDA AWARD WINNER.

Red-tailed hawk, Lamoille, Nevada. With eyesight eight times more powerful than a human's, this raptor seeks out snakes and small rodents. A full-grown female can weigh four pounds and have a fifty-six-inch wingspan. Photo © Cynthia A. Delaney

Coyote, Joshua Tree National Park. Smart and adaptable, coyotes survive across the U.S. expanding into urban areas. Hunting day and night, they can run more than thirty miles an hour and climb eight-foot fences. They will eat whatever is available. Night howling is communication and a way of calling out territorial boundaries. Photo © Cynthia A. Delaney

In plain sight

They are camouflaged hunters whose survival depends on their ability to find and overcome their prey. The hawk perches high in open country. The coyote slinks close to cover. The rattler seeks a warm spot to coil. They are always near, always hungry and alert, hiding in plain sight to trap the unwary.

BARBARA WIES, 2005

Western Rattlesnake, Great Basin. Shy, sun-loving and defensive, rattlers will climb small bushes seeking sun. Young are born live and lethal. Rattlers do not always warn before they strike, but they do control almost a quarter of the rodent population.
Photo © Jim Morgan

"For many of us, the horse is a symbol of what is right with the world. In spite of generations of careful breeding, the horse still seems to be a step or two out of the wild. In spite of training and confinement, the horse at a gallop seems to be a step or two from freedom."

SHARON B. SMITH
"THE AFFORDABLE HORSE"
HOWELL, 1994

A herd of Bruce and Mary Agar's horses runs freely on their remote Huntington, Oregon, ranch near the Idaho border.
Photo © Larry Turner

"Someday we would have boyfriends, husbands, children, careers—that's what the horses are substitutes for," according to adult theorists. "But what truly horsey girls discover in the end is that boyfriends, husbands, children and careers are the substitutes—for horses."

JANE SMILEY
"A YEAR AT THE RACES"
KNOPF, 2004

"Cappy (Rebs Captain Easy) was bred to run, but he didn't get to (or have to), thanks to me. He was a good colt." Photo © Jay Dusard

*Carol Kirby whispers to blue roan stud Sammy at the Lazy K Bar
Ranch in south central Montana. Maybe it's something Carol says,
but all of Sammy's offspring seem to inherit his good nature.
Photo © Barbara Van Cleve*

Pine Forest Mountains,
Humboldt County, Nevada.
Photo © Linda Dufurrena

"*Is it any wonder that we still marvel at the coming of each full moon, that it makes us restless, uncertain and adventurous? Is it any wonder, even though we no longer depend on it for good or evil omens, no longer govern our lives by its appearance, that it continues to arouse strange and indefinable feelings within us? As moderns we may have forgotten its ancient meaning, but inherently our responses to moonlight are no different from those of our ancestors—or, for that matter, from the responses of all other living things on the planet. It is still an event of cosmic significance.*"

SIGURD F. OLSON, "THE SINGING WILDERNESS," KNOPF, 1956

Sheepherder reads by kerosene lantern at Dufurrena Sheep Camp, Bilk Creek Mountains, Humboldt County, Nevada. Photo © Linda Dufurrena

"The [Basque] hotelkeepers—hoteleruak—were like priests, protecting the herders especially if they were in from Europe or from another state. Goodness of heart was involved, but money was the major factor. The hoteleruak let the herders run up tabs between jobs and paid their medical bills; even advanced cash. It was to the interest of the hotelkeeper to match herder and grower sucessfully."

LOUIS IRIGARAY, "A SHEPHERD WATCHES, A SHEPHERD SINGS,"
DOUBLEDAY, 1977

Nevada's Winnemucca Hotel was built in 1863 to be a refuge for the Basque sheepherders who spent most of the year roaming the hills with their bands of sheep. Basque hotels were where bachelor herders could receive letters from the old country, drink a Picon punch, and have a hearty meal. The hotels were home for the herders, who planned to return to the Basque country someday.

Miguel "Big Mike" Olano came to the U.S. from the Basque country in 1948 and bought the Winnemucca

Hotel in 1963. He still serves potent Picon punches at the massive, ornate bar that came around Cape Horn in the 1800s.

From the kitchen, Big Mike and Margaret's son, Mike, serves up family-style Basque meals—soup, salad, fresh bread, pasta, oxtail stew, juicy steaks, lamb shanks, platters of French fries, carafes of red wine and gallons of hot coffee. It is not only filling but inexpensive. And it is real Basque hospitality. *Photo © Larry Angier*

"And here I say to parents, and especially to wealthy parents, don't give your son money. As far as you can afford it, give him horses. No one ever came to grief—except honourable grief— through riding horses. No hour of life is lost that is spent in the saddle."

SIR WINSTON CHURCHILL,
STATESMAN,
PRIME MINISTER OF
GREAT BRITAIN,
1940-45, 1951-55

Brewing storm. On the east slope of the Crazy Mountains in central Montana, storm clouds billow from the vicinity of Yellowstone Park. The clouds silhouette a herd of horses being gathered for their move to a fresh pasture. Photo © Barbara Van Cleve

Big teeth, blue sky, Jackson Springs, Montana.
Photo © Cynthia Baldauf

"When I hear somebody talk about a horse
or a cow being stupid, I figure it's a sure sign
that animal has outfoxed them."

TOM DORRANCE, TRAINER AND AUTHOR OF "TRUE UNITY"
WORD DANCER PRESS, 1994

Horsing around. This one is hoping to crash the patio party at the Howard Taylor Ranch, Plymouth, California. Photo © Carolyn Fox

Ranchers hobble horses that are resting so they don't run off. This horse is yawning, eager to express an opinion during branding on a ranch in the Nebraska Sandhills. Photo © Joel Sartore

Appaloosa ranch horse, Tulelake, California.
Photo © Larry Turner

Spirit
Photographers
Writers
& Artists

PHOTOGRAPHERS

WRITERS

ARTISTS